Words in Flight

An Introduction to Poetry

Words in Flight

An Introduction to Poetry

Richard Abcarian
California State University, Northridge

Wadsworth Publishing Company, Inc.
Belmont, California

ISBN-0-534-00147-5
L. C. Cat. Card No. 79-181898
Printed in the United States of America

5 6 7 8 9 10–77

PS
584
.A2

. . . every improvement, and particularly every improvement made possible by mechanical invention, exacts its price, as we are discovering in our increasingly mechanized country. Often the price is exacted at the cost of nature and sometimes even at the cost of human nature. We are deluged with facts, but we have lost, or are losing, our human ability to feel them. Poetry still survives with us, survives with vigor and inventiveness, throwing up new masters capable of standing with the old. But the poem itself has lost its power in men's minds. We have not discarded the art as Herbert Spencer thought men would when the machine had come to flower, but we have impaired the practice of the skill the art can give, the skill of feeling truly and so truly knowing. We know with the head now, by the facts, by the abstractions. We seem unable to know as Shakespeare knew, who makes King Lear cry out to blinded Gloucester on the heath, "you see how this world goes," and Gloucester answers, "I see it feelingly."

—Archibald MacLeish, "Poetry and Journalism," from the Gideon Seymour Memorial Lecture Series

And wisdom is a butterfly
And not a gloomy bird of prey.

—W. B. Yeats

Preface

This anthology is based on the assumption that poetry does well on its own, that the joy, excitement, and power of poetry we talk so much about are more likely to be experienced by the student the less we talk about them, at least on the unchanging printed page. If we believe that what is said is inseparable from the way it is said, we must conclude also that poetry texts heavy on analysis and definition cannot convey to beginning students of poetry what they should. We ought not to be too concerned that students will miss something nor, indeed should we try to forestall erroneous interpretations (which often provide the instructor—the live instructor—with some of his best teaching material). There is, therefore, little analysis of individual poems in this anthology.

The book begins with the traditional question "What is poetry?" but after brief introductory remarks turns the question over to the poets themselves. Chapter Two, "The Words of Poetry," brings together a diverse group of poems that lend themselves to showing how the poet uses individual words and word patterns. Chapter Three, "The Strategies of Poetry," comprises poems that employ one or more of the common poetic devices (symbolism, metaphor, irony). If the instructor wishes, he may take up these three chapters in sequence, although the three together or each separately allow the instructor and the class whatever flexibility they wish.

Chapter Four, "Poems for Comparison and Evaluation," is made up of groups of poems similar in theme or technique. With insights and analytic tools acquired in the first three chapters, the student may now move to applying, refining, and enriching his understanding and appreciation of poems. But even at this stage, students in introductory courses experience difficulties, especially in evaluating poems. They find themselves like the man who was asked by a friend how his wife was and replied, "Compared to what?" The group of poems in this section illuminate one another, giving the student a basis for comparison and, thereby, evaluation.

Chapter Five, "Poetry and the Fine Arts," might be considered material for the study of poetic inspiration. Happily innocent of new critical scruples, students almost always express curiosity about the sources of poems. The instructor in many cases must reply that the specific inspiration is unknown or difficult to discover — even by the poet himself. Here is a group of poems inspired by paintings and sculpture, affording the student an opportunity to examine the specific inspiration. Discussions of these poems and paintings will no doubt raise many interesting issues, such as poetry-as-art criticism or the relationship between temporal and spatial art.

Chapter Six, "Poetry, Sound, and Music," breaks the silence of the printed page by joining words to sounds. The value of hearing poetry read by the poet or by a professional reader needs no comment; most instructors make an effort to play poetry recordings from time to time. But words are not only spoken but often sung to the accompaniment of instrumental music. This section includes poems that are sometimes set to music as well as the lyrics of some recent popular songs. (The recorded sources are listed after each poem or song.) Whether these lyrics qualify as great or even good poetry is unimportant (although many of them fare surprisingly well under analysis) compared to the advantages of trying to understand what happens when words are joined to music.

Chapter Seven offers examples of poets' revisions and early versions of poems along with the final version. A cursory look at this section will disabuse students of the notion that poets simply spill out finished poems. More detailed examinations can yield fascinating insights into the way a poet works and lead to a fuller understanding of the finished poem.

A Glossary of the most important and useful terms used in poetic analysis will be found at the end of the anthology. It has been placed there in order to provide more flexibility: the instructor may introduce terms in whatever order and at whatever pace seems best for the class.

My sincere thanks go to the following reviewers: Thomas L. Erskine, University of Delaware; Wallace Graves, San Fernando Valley State College; Geoffrey Marshall, University of Oklahoma.

Contents

Words in Flight

An Introduction to Poetry

One

What Is Poetry?

Poetry, someone once remarked, is the kind of writing where the lines don't end at the same place on the righthand side of the page. This definition will not serve, of course, but it does have an attractive simplicity for anyone who has tried to define poetry. Most of us, if we had to formulate a definition, would probably emphasize rhyme and rhythmic regularity and perhaps add something about inverted or unusual word order. But we wouldn't have to read very far (in fact no farther than the first poem in this anthology) to discover that some poems do not rely at all on rhyme and rhythmic regularity.

Nor are we helped much if we try to define poetry by subject matter. Love and death are perennial subjects for poets, for they are among the most profound and enduring aspects of man's existence. So are religion, politics, time, and brotherhood, to name but a few more. But any anthology of poetry will quickly demonstrate that the subject matter of poetry is as rich and varied as the mind and world of man. Spiders and herons, dukes and cities, even teaching poetry are also subjects of poetry.

The problem, then, is that the abstract statement of subject matter bears about as much relationship to individual poems as the abstract concept *human experience* bears to a living individual. True, John Donne's "A Valediction: Forbidding Mourning" (p. 51) and Andrew Marvell's "To His Coy Mistress" (p. 50) are both about love, but to so characterize them scarcely does justice to the radically different treatment of love in the two poems.

Perhaps the best approach to poetry is not to worry over the question of its essential nature. Whatever it is, poetry is one of the most ancient and enduring

1

uses to which man has put language; there is scarcely a culture or a period in man's recorded history when he has not written and read poetry. If we want to generalize about poetry, it would be safe to say that man cannot or will not live without it. Whether we consider it a form of exploration, communication, or discovery, it seems to serve certain fundamental human needs in a way nothing else can.

It would be futile to attempt a catalogue of the human needs that poetry serves. They range from the pleasures of rhythm and the startling use of words or phrases to the delight we take in the total structure of the poem, the satisfaction of perceiving the mastery of an emotion or experience or idea. The pleasures of poetry derive from many sources and levels, some of them closely related to the pleasure we take in working crossword puzzles, reciting simple nursery rhymes, or watching skilled tennis players. It is important that we bear this in mind, that we not come to poetry with the feeling that it is a high mystery, unrelated to anything else we do or like, created by a few strange people in order to ensure English professors a livelihood.

"All that matters about poetry," Dylan Thomas once remarked, "is the enjoyment of it, however tragic it may be; all that matters is the eternal movement behind it, the great undercurrent of human grief, folly, pretension, exaltation, and ignorance, however unlofty the intention of the poem." It is in this spirit that we ought to approach poetry. The analysis and study of poems and poetic devices ought not to be an arid intellectual exercise but a means of enhancing our understanding and thus our enjoyment of poems. Of course there is no guarantee we shall be rewarded for the effort. We may spend a great deal of time analyzing a poem and achieving a full understanding of it—only to find that we do not enjoy it. Our different temperaments, interests, experiences, and tastes determine the poems we enjoy and those we do not. "I like to read only the poets I like," Dylan Thomas also said, but added the important explanation that "this means that I have to read a lot of poems I don't like before I find the ones I do. . . ."

This does not mean that we should abandon ourselves to completely subjective standards in dealing with poetry. It is possible to formulate reasonably objective criteria about poetry that will allow us to discuss at least some of the reasons a particular poem does or does not give us enjoyment. Some of those criteria you will no doubt begin to define for yourself as you read more and more poems. You will probably even begin to formulate some sort of general definition of what poetry is. But discussions with your fellow students and your instructor— or anyone else interested in talking with you about poems—will reveal general areas of agreement while at the same time pointing up the dangers of becoming too rigid or dogmatic on the subject. The following poems should help you begin your study of poetry; they should also demonstrate the impossibility of arriving at a single clear, acceptable definition of poetry.

For Saundra

Nikki Giovanni (1943–   )

i wanted to write
a poem
that rhymes
but revolution doesn't lend
itself to be-bopping   5

then my neighbor
who thinks i hate
asked — do you ever write
tree poems — i like trees
so i thought   10

i'll write a beautiful green tree poem
peeked from my window
to check the image
noticed the school yard was covered
with asphalt   15
no green — no trees grow
in manhattan

then, well, i thought the sky
i'll do a big blue sky poem
but all the clouds have winged   20
low since no-Dick was elected

so i thought again
and it occurred to me
maybe i shouldn't write
at all   25
but clean my gun
and check my kerosene supply

perhaps these are not poetic
times
at all   30

today is a day of great joy

Victor Hernandez Cruz (1949–   )

when they stop poems
in the mail & clap
their hands & dance to
them
when women become pregnant   5
by the side of poems
the strongest sounds making
the river go along

it is a great day

as poems fall down to   10
movie crowds in restaurants
in bars

when poems start to
knock down walls to
choke politicians   15
when poems scream &
begin to break the air

that is the time of
true poets that is
the time of greatness   20

a true poet aiming
poems & watching things
fall to the ground

it is a great day.

In a Spring Still Not Written of

Robert Wallace (1932–   )

This morning
with a class of girls outdoors, I saw
how frail poems are
in a world burning up with flowers,
in which, overhead,   5
the great elms
— green, and tall —
stood carrying leaves in their arms.

The girls listened equally
to my drone, reading, and to the bees'   10
ricocheting
among them for the blossom on the bone,
or gazed off at a distant mower's
astronomies of green
and clover, flashing,   15
threshing in the new, untarnished sunlight.

And all the while, dwindling,
tinier, the voices — Yeats, Marvell, Donne —
sank drowning
in a spring still not written of,   20
as only the sky
clear above the brick bell-tower
— blue, and white —
was shifting toward the hour.

Calm, indifferent, cross-legged   25
or on elbows half-lying in the grass —
how should the great dead
tell them of dying?
They will come to time for poems at last,
when they have found they are no more   30
the beautiful and young
all poems are for.

Adam's Curse

W. B. Yeats (1865–1939)

We sat together at one summer's end,
That beautiful mild woman, your close friend,
And you and I, and talked of poetry.
I said, 'A line will take us hours maybe;
Yet if it does not seem a moment's thought,   5
Our stitching and unstitching has been naught.

Better go down upon your marrow-bones
And scrub a kitchen pavement, or break stones
Like an old pauper, in all kinds of weather;
For to articulate sweet sounds together   10
Is to work harder than all these, and yet
Be thought an idler by the noisy set
Of bankers, schoolmasters, and clergymen
The martyrs call the world.'

                              And thereupon
That beautiful mild woman for whose sake   15
There's many a one shall find out all heartache
On finding that her voice is sweet and low
Replied, 'To be born woman is to know—
Although they do not talk of it at school—
That we must labour to be beautiful.'   20

I said, 'It's certain there is no fine thing
Since Adam's fall but needs much labouring.
There have been lovers who thought love should be
So much compounded of high courtesy
That they would sigh and quote with learned looks   25
Precedents out of beautiful old books;
Yet now it seems an idle trade enough.'

We sat grown quiet at the name of love;
We saw the last embers of daylight die,
And in the trembling blue-green of the sky   30
A moon, worn as if it had been a shell
Washed by time's waters as they rose and fell
About the stars and broke in days and years.

6

I had a thought for no one's but your ears:
That you were beautiful, and that I strove   35
To love you in the old high way of love;
That it had all seemed happy, and yet we'd grown
As weary-hearted as that hollow moon.

Poetry

Marianne Moore (1887–1972)

I, too, dislike it: there are things that are important beyond all this fiddle.
    Reading it, however, with a perfect contempt for it, one discovers in
    it after all, a place for the genuine.
        Hands that can grasp, eyes
        that can dilate, hair that can rise   5
            if it must, these things are important not because a

high-sounding interpretation can be put upon them but because they are
    useful. When they become so derivative as to become unintelligible,
    the same thing may be said for all of us, that we
        do not admire what   10
        we cannot understand: the bat
            holding on upside down or in quest of something to

eat, elephants pushing, a wild horse taking a roll, a tireless wolf under
    a tree, the immovable critic twitching his skin like a horse that feels
        a flea, the base-   15
    ball fan, the statistician —
        nor is it valid
            to discriminate against "business documents and

school-books"; all these phenomena are important. One must make a
        distinction
    however: when dragged into prominence by half poets, the result is
        not poetry,   20
    nor till the poets among us can be
        "literalists of
        the imagination" — above
            insolence and triviality and can present

for inspection, "imaginary gardens with real toads in them," shall we   25
    have it. In the meantime, if you demand on the one hand,
  the raw material of poetry in
    all its rawness and
    that which is on the other hand
      genuine, you are interested in poetry.   30

Ars Poetica

Archibald MacLeish (1892–   )

A poem should be palpable and mute
As a globed fruit,

Dumb
As old medallions to the thumb,

Silent as the sleeve-worn stone   5
Of casement ledges where the moss has grown —

A poem should be wordless
As the flight of birds.

A poem should be motionless in time
As the moon climbs,   10

Leaving, as the moon releases
Twig by twig the night-entangled trees,

Leaving, as the moon behind the winter leaves,
Memory by memory the mind —

A poem should be motionless in time   15
As the moon climbs

A poem should be equal to:
Not true

For all the history of grief
An empty doorway and a maple leaf   20

For love
The leaning grasses and the two lights above the sea—

A poem should not mean
But be

Pitcher

Robert Francis (1901–   )

His art is eccentricity, his aim
How not to hit the mark he seems to aim at,

His passion how to avoid the obvious,
His technique how to vary the avoidance.

The others throw to be comprehended. He   5
Throws to be a moment misunderstood.

Yet not too much. Not errant, arrant, wild,
But every seeming aberration willed.

Not to, yet still, still to communicate
Making the batter understand too late.   10

Catch

Robert Francis (1901–   )

Two boys uncoached are tossing a poem together,
Overhand, underhand, backhand, sleight of hand, every hand,
Teasing with attitudes, latitudes, interludes, altitudes,
High, make him fly off the ground for it, low, make him stoop,
Make him scoop it up, make him as-almost-as-possible miss it,   5
Fast, let him sting from it, now, now fool him slowly,
Anything, everything, tricky, risky, nonchalant,

9

Anything under the sun to outwit the prosy,
Over the tree and the long sweet cadence down,
Over his head, make him scramble to pick up the meaning,   10
And now, like a posy, a pretty one plump in his hands.

[Not marble, nor the gilded monuments]

William Shakespeare (1564–1616)

Not marble, nor the gilded monuments
Of princes, shall outlive this powerful rhyme;
But you shall shine more bright in these contents
Than unswept stone besmeared with sluttish time.
When wasteful war shall statues overturn,   5
And broils root out the work of masonry,
Nor Mars his sword nor war's quick fire shall burn
The living record of your memory.
'Gainst death and all-oblivious enmity
Shall you pace forth; your praise shall still find room   10
Even in the eyes of all posterity
That wear this world out to the ending doom.
So, till the judgment that yourself arise,
You live in this, and dwell in lovers' eyes.

"Not Marble, Nor the Gilded Monuments"

Archibald MacLeish (1892–   )

For Adele

The praisers of women in their proud and beautiful poems,
Naming the grave mouth and the hair and the eyes,
Boasted those they loved should be forever remembered:
These were lies.

The words sound but the face in the Istrian sun is forgotten.   5
The poet speaks but to her dead ears no more.
The sleek throat is gone — and the breast that was troubled to listen:
Shadow from door.

Therefore I will not praise your knees nor your fine walking,
Telling you men shall remember your name as long   10
As lips move or breath is spent or the iron of English
Rings from a tongue.

I shall say you were young, and your arms straight, and your mouth scarlet:
I shall say you will die and none will remember you:
Your arms change, and none remember the swish of your garments,   15
Nor the click of your shoe.

Not with my hand's strength, not with difficult labor
Springing the obstinate words to the bones of your breast
And the stubborn line to your young stride and the breath to your breathing
And the beat to your haste   20
Shall I prevail on the hearts of unborn to remember.

(What is a dead girl but a shadowy ghost
Or a dead man's voice but a distant and vain affirmation
Like dream words most)

Therefore I will not speak of the undying glory of women.   25
I will say you were young and straight and your skin fair
And you stood in the door and the sun was a shadow of leaves on your shoulders
And a leaf on your hair —

I will not speak of the famous beauty of dead women:
I will say the shape of a leaf lay once on your hair.   30
Till the world ends and the eyes are out and the mouths broken
Look! It is there!

[Constantly risking absurdity]

Lawrence Ferlinghetti (1919–   )

    Constantly risking absurdity
                  and death
       whenever he performs
            above the heads
                  of his audience   5

                    the poet like an acrobat
                                climbs on rime
                            to a high wire of his own making
and balancing on eyebeams
                            above a sea of faces   10
            paces his way
                        to the other side of day
        performing entrechats
                        and sleight-of-foot tricks
and other high theatrics   15
                            and all without mistaking
                any thing
                        for what it may not be

    For he's the super realist
                            who must perforce perceive   20
                taut truth
                            before the taking of each stance or step
    in his supposed advance
                            toward that still higher perch
where Beauty stands and waits   25
                            with gravity
                                to start her death-defying leap

    And he
            a little charleychaplin man
                            who may or may not catch   30
            her fair eternal form
                            spreadeagled in the empty air
            of existence

In Memory of W. B. Yeats

W. H. Auden (1907–   )

                                I

He disappeared in the dead of winter:
The brooks were frozen, the airports almost deserted,
And snow disfigured the public statues;
The mercury sank in the mouth of the dying day.
What instruments we have agree   5
The day of his death was a dark cold day.

Far from his illness
The wolves ran on through the evergreen forests,
The peasant river was untempted by the fashionable quays;
By mourning tongues   10
The death of the poet was kept from his poems.

But for him it was his last afternoon as himself,
An afternoon of nurses and rumours;
The provinces of his body revolted,
The squares of his mind were empty,   15
Silence invaded the suburbs,
The current of his feeling failed: he became his admirers.

Now he is scattered among a hundred cities
And wholly given over to unfamiliar affections,
To find his happiness in another kind of wood   20
And be punished under a foreign code of conscience.
The words of a dead man
Are modified in the guts of the living.

But in the importance and noise of to-morrow
When the brokers are roaring like beasts on the floor of the Bourse,   25
And the poor have the sufferings to which they are fairly accustomed,
And each in the cell of himself is almost convinced of his freedom,
A few thousand will think of this day
As one thinks of a day when one did something slightly unusual.

What instruments we have agree   30
The day of his death was a dark cold day.

II

You were silly like us: your gift survived it all:
The parish of rich women, physical decay,
Yourself. Mad Ireland hurt you into poetry.
Now Ireland has her madness and her weather still,   35
For poetry makes nothing happen: it survives
In the valley of its making where executives
Would never want to tamper, flows on south
From ranches of isolation and the busy griefs,
Raw towns that we believe and die in; it survives,   40
A way of happening, a mouth.

III

Earth, receive an honoured guest:
William Yeats is laid to rest.
Let the Irish vessel lie
Emptied of its poetry.   45

13

In the nightmare of the dark
All the dogs of Europe bark,
And the living nations wait,
Each sequestered in its hate;

Intellectual disgrace   50
Stares from every human face,
And the seas of pity lie
Locked and frozen in each eye.

Follow, poet, follow right
To the bottom of the night,   55
With your unconstraining voice
Still persuade us to rejoice;

With the farming of a verse
Make a vineyard of the curse,
Sing of human unsuccess   60
In a rapture of distress;

In the deserts of the heart
Let the healing fountain start,
In the prison of his days
Teach the free man how to praise.   65

In My Craft or Sullen Art

Dylan Thomas (1914–1953)

In my craft or sullen art
Exercised in the still night
When only the moon rages
And the lovers lie abed
With all their griefs in their arms,   5
I labor by singing light
Not for ambition or bread
Or the strut and trade of charms
On the ivory stages
But for the common wages   10
Of their most secret heart.

Not for the proud man apart
From the raging moon I write
On these spindrift pages
Nor for the towering dead   15
With their nightingales and psalms
But for the lovers, their arms
Round the griefs of the ages,
Who pay no praise or wages
Nor heed my craft or art.   20

Variations: # 21

James Stephens (1882–1950)

Nothing is easy! Pity then
The poet more than other men:

And, since his aim is ecstasy,
And, since none work so hard as he,
Forgive the poet poesy!   5

He hath the same dull eyes: his ears
Are dull-attuned: his hopes and fears
Are those same ravening dogs that bay
The moon, and bury bones in clay!

Tho' he on offals, too, was bred,   10
Tho' in his heart, and in his head
The brute doth slaver, yet he can
Banish the brute from off the man,
The man from that beyond the man.

He gave a song, a wing, to words   15
That they might fly and sing like birds
In love, who cannot too much sing
The heaven, the earth, the everything;
And love, the air that buoys along
The wing, the singer, and the song.   20

"Variations: #21" reprinted with permission of The Macmillan Company, Mrs. Iris Wise, Macmillan London & Basingstoke, and The Macmillan Company of Canada Limited from *Collected Poems* by James Stephens. Copyright 1930 by The Macmillan Company, renewed 1958 by Cynthia Stephens.

Yea, wonder is that he hath done,
For all that is beneath the sun
By magic he transfigures to
A better sound, a finer view:
And — loveliest tale of all that's true!   25
He tells that you come to the spring,
And that the spring returns to you.

Verse

Oliver St. John Gogarty (1878–1957)

What should we know,
For better or worse,
Of the Long Ago,
Were it not for Verse:
What ships went down;   5
What walls were razed;
Who won the crown;
What lads were praised?
A fallen stone,
Or a waste of sands;   10
And all is known
Of Art-less lands.
But you need not delve
By the Sea-side hills
Where the Muse herself   15
All Time fulfills,
Who cuts with his scythe
All things but hers;
All but the blithe
Hexameters.   20

Ode

Arthur O'Shaughnessy (1844–1881)

We are the music-makers
   And we are the dreamers of dreams,
Wandering by lone sea-breakers,
   And sitting by desolate streams; —
World-losers and world-forsakers,   5
   On whom the pale moon gleams:
Yet we are the movers and shakers
   Of the world for ever, it seems.

With wonderful deathless ditties
We build up the world's great cities,   10
   And out of a fabulous story
   We fashion an empire's glory:
One man with a dream, at pleasure,
   Shall go forth and conquer a crown;
And three with a new song's measure   15
   Can trample an empire down.

We, in the ages lying
   In the buried past of the earth,
Built Nineveh with our sighing,
   And Babel itself with our mirth;   20
And o'erthrew them with prophesying,
   To the old of the new world's worth;
For each age is a dream that is dying,
   Or one that is coming to birth.

A Poet's Progress

Michael Hamburger (1924–   )

Like snooker balls thrown on the table's faded green,
rare ivory and weighted with his best ambitions,
at first his words are launched: not certain what they mean,
he loves to see them roll, rebound, assume positions
which — since not he — some higher power has assigned.   5

"A Poet's Progress," originally published in *Flowering Cactus*, The Hand and Flower Press, Oldington, Kent, 1950. Copyright by Michael Hamburger. Reprinted by permission of Michael Hamburger.

17

ne begins: dead players, living critics
n — and suddenly one eye goes blind,
lds the cue shakes like a paralytic's,
g, every clinking sound portends
        defeat. Amazed, he finds that still   10
it is not he who guides his missiles to their ends
but an unkind geometry that mocks his will.

If he persists, for years he'll practice patiently,
lock all the doors, learn all the tricks, keep noises out,
though he may pick a ghost or two for company   15
or pierce the room's inhuman silence with a shout.
More often silence wins; then soon the green felt seems
an evil playground, lawless, lost to time, forsaken,
and he a fool caught in the water weeds of dreams
whom only death or frantic effort can awaken.   20

At last, a master player, he can face applause,
looks for a fit opponent, former friends, emerges;
but no one knows him now. He questions his own cause
and has forgotten why he yielded to those urges,
took up a wooden cue to strike a coloured ball.   25
Wise now, he goes on playing; both his house and heart
unguarded solitudes, hospitable to all
who can endure the cold intensity of art.

Of Modern Poetry

Wallace Stevens (1879–1955)

The poem of the mind in the act of finding
What will suffice. It has not always had
To find: the scene was set; it repeated what
Was in the script.
                    Then the theatre was changed
To something else. Its past was a souvenir.   5
It has to be living, to learn the speech of the place.
It has to face the men of the time and to meet
The women of the time. It has to think about war
And it has to find what will suffice. It has
To construct a new stage. It has to be on that stage   10

And, like an insatiable actor, slowly and
With meditation, speak words that in the ear,
In the delicatest ear of the mind, repeat,
Exactly, that which it wants to hear, at the sound
Of which, an invisible audience listens,   15
Not to the play, but to itself, expressed
In an emotion as of two people, as of two
Emotions becoming one. The actor is
A metaphysician in the dark, twanging
An instrument, twanging a wiry string that gives   20
Sounds passing through sudden rightnesses, wholly
Containing the mind, below which it cannot descend,
Beyond which it has no will to rise.
                                                        It must
Be the finding of a satisfaction, and may
Be of a man skating, a woman dancing, a woman   25
Combing. The poem of the act of the mind.

Poem about a Poem about a Poem

Robert Conquest (1917–   )

". . . often writes not about life but poetry" —
                                        [a critic]

To gallop horses (or eat buns)
    Is Life, and may be Song,
(To sink drains or interpret dreams
Or listen to a Baby's screams)
But not to write a poem, it seems.   5
        That isn't Life, it's wrong.

And yet — at least I thought so once
        The time I wrote those lines —
To ride a verse is quite a thing,
(Sinking a rhyme, interpreting   10
The wordless cry, the concept's ring.
        The field of sensuous signs.)

"Poem about a Poem about a Poem" reprinted from the London *Times Literary Supplement*, September 8, 1961, by permission of Robert Conquest.

But let the bays, the greys, the duns
    Go pounding round the course.
Stallions may sometimes turn vicious.   15
But art gets so damned meretricious.
Yes, horses are better than wishes:
    I wish I had a horse.

Ten Definitions of Poetry

Carl Sandburg (1878–1967)

1 Poetry is a projection across silence of cadences arranged to break the silence with definite intentions of echoes, syllables, wave lengths.
2 Poetry is the journal of a sea animal living on land, wanting to fly the air.
3 Poetry is a series of explanations of life, fading off into horizons too swift for explanations.
4 Poetry is a search for syllables to shoot at the barriers of the unknown and the unknowable.
5 Poetry is a theorem of a yellow-silk handkerchief knotted with riddles, sealed in a balloon tied to the tail of a kite flying in a white wind against a blue sky in spring.
6 Poetry is the silence and speech between a wet struggling root of a flower and a sunlit blossom of that flower.
7 Poetry is the harnessing of the paradox of earth cradling life and then entombing it.
8 Poetry is a phantom script telling how rainbows are made and why they go away.
9 Poetry is the synthesis of hyacinths and biscuits.
10 Poetry is the opening and closing of a door, leaving those who look through to guess about what is seen during a moment.

Preface to the Picture of Dorian Gray

Oscar Wilde (1856–1900)

The artist is the creator of beautiful things.
To reveal art and conceal the artist is art's aim.
The critic is he who can translate into another manner or a new material his impression of beautiful things.

The highest, as the lowest, form of criticism is a mode of
autobiography.
Those who find ugly meaning in beautiful things are corrupt without being
  charming. This is a fault.   5
      Those who find beautiful meanings in beautiful things are
      the cultivated. For these there is hope.
  They are the elect to whom beautiful things mean only Beauty.
  There is no such thing as a moral or an immoral book.
  Books are well written, or badly written. That is all.
The nineteenth-century dislike of Realism is the rage of Caliban seeing his own
  face in a glass.   10
      The nineteenth-century dislike of Romanticism is the rage of Caliban
      not seeing his own face in a glass.
  The moral life of man forms part of the subject matter of the artist, but the
  morality of art consists in the perfect use of an imperfect medium. No artist
  desires to prove anything. Even things that are true can be proved.
  No artist has ethical sympathies. An ethical sympathy in an artist is an un-
  pardonable mannerism of style.
      No artist is ever morbid. The artist can express everything.
Thought and language are to the artist instruments of an art.   15
  Vice and virtue are to the artist materials for an art.
From the point of view of form, the type of all the arts is the art of the musician.
From the point of view of feeling, the actor's craft is the type.
      All art is at once surface and symbol.
  Those who go beneath the surface do so at their peril.   20
      Those who read the symbol do so at their peril.
It is the spectator, and not life, that art really mirrors.
Diversity of opinion about a work of art shows that the work is new, complex,
  and vital.
      When critics disagree the artist is in accord with himself.
We can forgive a man for making a useful thing as long as he does not
  admire it.   25
The only excuse for making a useless thing is that one admires it intensely.
  All art is quite useless.

Two

The Words of Poetry

"In reading prose," Ralph Waldo Emerson remarked, "I am sensitive as soon as a sentence drags; but in poetry, as soon as one word drags." Though we may not all be as sensitive as Emerson, his remark serves to suggest how important the words of poetry are. A writer of prose may from time to time ignore or slight the problem of diction, confident that his ideas will be clear enough in any case. A brilliant sociologist or literary critic may be a mediocre writer. But when a poet writes badly, he is a poor poet; if his words drag, his poem drags.

If we are to understand and appreciate poems, we must develop something of the same sensitivity to words. And we acquire it not simply that we may detect when words drag, though this kind of critical judgment is valuable. More important are the positive benefits: a sensitivity to words not only allows us to experience the full and subtle richness of poems but also provides often the most fruitful way into the theme of a poem.

The poems in this chapter can be considered in terms of key words and word patterns. This approach — in fact, any approach that isolates one element — can be useful in developing our awareness. The poet's medium is language and the smallest unit of language is the word. It is therefore sensible to begin with a consideration of words.

As you read, your attention may be drawn to words that seem unusual or especially apt. The dictionary is indispensable not only for the obvious purpose of providing definitions of words you may not know but also in revealing that there is much more to the poet's use of the words you do know. For example, if you are unfamiliar with the word "descant" in the fifth line of Yeats's "After

Long Silence" (p. 26), you will have to look it up in the dictionary; the dictionary will also help you to understand why "descant" is a better choice in the poem than a more familiar word like "converse." Or, again, the dictionary will help you to understand how rich the meanings of "ban" are in the seventh line of Blake's "London" (p. 31).

There are limits to the usefulness of the dictionary, however. It will not help you to understand why in the final line of Hardy's "The Ruined Maid" (p. 25) 'Melia lapses from her proper speech into "ain't." Only a sensitivity to words can tell you that, or help you to recognize the pattern of legal terms in Shakespeare's sonnet (p. 31) or of official, bureaucratic terms in cummings's "i sing of Olaf" (p. 35). The word "leafmeal" in the eighth line of Hopkins's "Spring and Fall" (p. 34) is not to be found in the dictionary; Hopkins is assuming his readers will recognize that he has invented a word on analogy with "piecemeal."

As you read through the poems in this chapter, dictionary in hand, you will make many discoveries about words. And you will probably discover in class that you failed to recognize the full significance of a good many words. It would be surprising indeed if your experience were otherwise. Sensitivity to words develops with time and effort. And good poems often reveal some new richness with each re-reading.

The Naked and the Nude

Robert Graves (1895–   )

For me, the naked and the nude
(By lexicographers construed
As synonyms that should express
The same deficiency of dress
Or shelter) stand as wide apart   5
As love from lies, or truth from art.

Lovers without reproach will gaze
On bodies naked and ablaze;
The hippocratic eye will see
In nakedness, anatomy;   10
And naked shines the Goddess when
She mounts her lion among men.

The nude are bold, the nude are sly
To hold each treasonable eye.
While draping by a showman's trick   15
Their dishabille in rhetoric,
They grin a mock-religious grin
Of scorn at those of naked skin.

The naked, *therefore,* who compete
Against the nude may know defeat;   20
Yet when they both together tread
The briary pastures of the dead,
By Gorgons with long whips pursued,
How naked go the sometime nude!

The Ruined Maid

Thomas Hardy (1840–1928)

"O 'Melia, my dear, this does everything crown!
Who could have supposed I should meet you in Town?
And whence such fair garments, such prosperi-ty?" —
"O didn't you know I'd been ruined?" said she.

— "You left us in tatters, without shoes or socks,   5
Tired of digging potatoes, and spudding up docks;
And now you've gay bracelets and bright feathers
        three!" —
"Yes: that's how we dress when we're ruined," said she.

— "At home in the barton you said 'thee' and 'thou,'
And 'thik oon,' and 'theäs oon,' and 't'other'; but now   10
Your talking quite fits 'ee for high compa-ny!" —
"Some polish is gained with one's ruin," said she.

— "Your hands were like paws then, your face blue and bleak
But now I'm bewitched by your delicate cheek,
And your little gloves fit as on any la-dy!" —   15
"We never do work when we're ruined," said she.

— "You used to call home-life a hag-ridden dream,
And you'd sigh, and you'd sock; but at present you
        seem
To know not of megrims or melancho-ly!" —
"True. One's pretty lively when ruined," said she.   20

"The Ruined Maid" from *Collected Poems of Thomas Hardy* reprinted by permission of The Macmillan Company, the Hardy Estate, Macmillan London & Basingstoke, and The Macmillan Company of Canada Limited.

25

—"I wish I had feathers, a fine sweeping gown,
And a delicate face, and could strut about Town!"—
"My dear—a raw country girl, such as you be,
Cannot quite expect that. You ain't ruined," said she.

spudding up docks (l. 6): digging up weeds.   barton (l. 9): farmyard.   megrims (l. 19):
low spirits.

Upon Julia's Clothes

Robert Herrick (1591–1674)

Whenas in silks my Julia goes,
Then, then, methinks, how sweetly flows
That liquefaction of her clothes.
Next, when I cast mine eyes and see
That brave vibration each way free,   5
Oh, how that glittering taketh me!

After Long Silence

W. B. Yeats (1865–1939)

Speech after long silence; it is right,
All other lovers being estranged or dead,
Unfriendly lamplight hid under its shade,
The curtains drawn upon unfriendly night,
That we descant and yet again descant   5
Upon the supreme theme of Art and Song:
Bodily decrepitude is wisdom; young
We loved each other and were ignorant.

Autumn

Roy Campbell (1901–1957)

I love to see, when leaves depart,
The clear anatomy arrive,
Winter, the paragon of art,
That kills all forms of life and feeling
Save what is pure and will survive.   5

Already now the clanging chains
Of geese are harnessed to the moon:
Stripped are the great sun-clouding planes:
And the dark pines, their own revealing,
Let in the needles of the noon.   10

Strained by the gale the olives whiten
Like hoary wrestlers bent with toil
And, with the vines, their branches lighten
To brim our vats where summer lingers
In the red froth and sun-gold oil.   15

Soon on our hearth's reviving pyre
Their rotted stems will crumble up:
And like a ruby, panting fire,
The grape will redden on your fingers
Through the lit crystal of the cup.   20

[There is no Frigate like a Book]

Emily Dickinson (1830–1886)

There is no Frigate like a Book
To take us Lands away
Nor any Coursers like a Page
Of prancing Poetry —
This Travel may the poorest take   5
Without offence of Toll —
How frugal is the Chariot
That bears the Human soul.

"Autumn" from *Adamastor* reprinted by permission of Curtis Brown Ltd.

"There is no Frigate like a Book" reprinted by permission of the publishers and the Trustees of Amherst College from Thomas H. Johnson, Editor, *The Poems of Emily Dickinson*, Cambridge, Mass.: The Belknap Press of Harvard University Press, copyright 1951, 1955 by The President and Fellows of Harvard College.

27

Naming of Parts

Henry Reed (1914–   )

To-day we have naming of parts. Yesterday,
We had daily cleaning. And to-morrow morning,
We shall have what to do after firing. But to-day,
To-day we have naming of parts. Japonica
Glistens like coral in all of the neighboring gardens,   5
   And to-day we have naming of parts.

This is the lower sling swivel. And this
Is the upper sling swivel, whose use you will see,
When you are given your slings. And this is the piling swivel,
Which in your case you have not got. The branches   10
Hold in the gardens their silent, eloquent gestures,
   Which in our case we have not got.

This is the safety-catch, which is always released
With an easy flick of the thumb. And please do not let me
See anyone using his finger. You can do it quite easy   15
If you have any strength in your thumb. The blossoms
Are fragile and motionless, never letting anyone see
   Any of them using their finger.

And this you can see is the bolt. The purpose of this
Is to open the breech, as you see. We can slide it   20
Rapidly backwards and forwards: we call this
Easing the spring. And rapidly backwards and forwards
The early bees are assaulting and fumbling the flowers:
   They call it easing the Spring.

They call it easing the Spring: it is perfectly easy   25
If you have any strength in your thumb: like the bolt,
And the breech, and the cocking-piece, and the point of balance,
Which in our case we have not got; and the almond-blossom
Silent in all of the gardens and the bees going backwards and forwards,
   For to-day we have naming of parts.   30

"Naming of Parts" from *A Map of Verona* reprinted by permission of Jonathan Cape Ltd. on behalf of Henry Reed.

Cargoes

John Masefield (1878–   )

Quinquireme of Nineveh from distant Ophir,
Rowing home to haven in sunny Palestine,
With a cargo of ivory,
And apes and peacocks,
Sandalwood, cedarwood, and sweet white wine.   5

Stately Spanish galleon coming from the Isthmus,
Dipping through the Tropics by the palm-green shores,
With a cargo of diamonds,
Emeralds, amethysts,
Topazes, and cinnamon, and gold moidores.   10

Dirty British coaster with a salt-caked smoke-stack,
Butting through the Channel in the mad March days,
With a cargo of Tyne coal,
Road-rails, pig-lead,
Firewood, iron-ware, and cheap tin trays.   15

To Helen

Edgar Allan Poe (1809–1849)

Helen, thy beauty is to me
  Like those Nicéan barks of yore,
That gently, o'er a perfumed sea,
  The weary, way-worn wanderer bore
  To his own native shore.   5

On desperate seas long wont to roam,
  Thy hyacinth hair, thy classic face,
Thy Naiad airs have brought me home
  To the glory that was Greece,
And the grandeur that was Rome.   10

"Cargoes" reprinted with permission of The Macmillan Company from *Poems* by John Masefield. Copyright 1912 by The Macmillan Company, renewed 1940 by John Masefield.

Lo! in yon brilliant window-niche
    How statue-like I see thee stand,
    The agate lamp within thy hand!
Ah, Psyche, from the regions which
    Are Holy-Land!   15

A Hymn to God the Father

John Donne (1572–1631)

Wilt Thou forgive that sin where I begun,
    Which is my sin, though it were done before?
Wilt Thou forgive those sins through which I run,
    And do them still, though still I do deplore?
        When Thou hast done, Thou hast not done,   5
            For I have more.

Wilt Thou forgive that sin by which I won
    Others to sin and made my sin their door?
Wilt Thou forgive that sin which I did shun
    A year or two, but wallowed in a score?   10
        When Thou hast done, Thou hast not done,
            For I have more.

I have a sin of fear, that when I have spun
    My last thread, I shall perish on the shore;
Swear by Thy self, that at my death Thy sun   15
    Shall shine as it shines now and heretofore;
        And, having done that, Thou hast done,
            I have no more.

On His Blindness

John Milton (1608–1674)

When I consider how my light is spent
    Ere half my days in this dark world and wide,
    And that one talent which is death to hide
    Lodged with me useless, though my soul more bent

30

To serve therewith my Maker, and present   5
    My true account, lest he returning chide.
    "Doth God exact day-labor, light denied?"
    I fondly ask. But Patience, to prevent
That murmur, soon replies, "God doth not need
    Either man's work or his own gifts. Who best   10
    Bear his mild yoke, they serve him best. His state
Is kingly: thousands at his bidding speed,
    And post o'er land and ocean without rest;
    They also serve who only stand and wait."

London

William Blake (1757–1827)

I wander through each chartered street,
Near where the chartered Thames does flow
And mark in every face I meet
Marks of weakness, marks of woe.

In every cry of every man,   5
In every infant's cry of fear,
In every voice; in every ban,
The mind-forged manacles I hear:

How the chimmney-sweeper's cry
Every blackening church appalls,   10
And the hapless soldier's sigh
Runs in blood down palace-walls.

But most, through midnight streets I hear
How the youthful harlot's curse
Blasts the new-born infant's tear,   15
And blights with plagues the marriage-hearse.

[When to the sessions of sweet silent thought]

William Shakespeare (1564–1616)

When to the sessions of sweet silent thought
I summon up remembrance of things past,
I sigh the lack of many a thing I sought,
And with old woes new wail my dear time's waste;

31

Then can I drown an eye, unused to flow,   5
For precious friends hid in death's dateless night,
And weep afresh love's long since cancelled woe,
And moan the expense of many a vanished sight.
Then can I grieve at grievances foregone,
And heavily from woe to woe tell o'er   10
The sad account of fore-bemoanèd moan,
Which I new pay as if not paid before:
      But if the while I think on thee, dear friend,
      All losses are restored, and sorrows end.

Fern Hill

Dylan Thomas (1914–1953)

Now as I was young and easy under the apple boughs
About the lilting house and happy as the grass was green,
      The night above the dingle starry,
            Time let me hail and climb
        Golden in the heydays of his eyes,   5
And honored among wagons I was prince of the apple towns
And once below a time I lordly had the trees and leaves
            Trail with daisies and barley
        Down the rivers of the windfall light.

And as I was green and carefree, famous among the barns   10
About the happy yard and singing as the farm was home,
      In the sun that is young once only,
            Time let me play and be
        Golden in the mercy of his means,
And green and golden I was huntsman and herdsman, the calves   15
Sang to my horn, the foxes on the hills barked clear and cold,
            And the sabbath rang slowly
        In the pebbles of the holy streams.

All the sun long it was running, it was lovely, the hay
Fields high as the house, the tunes from the chimneys, it was air   20
      And playing, lovely and watery
            And fire green as grass.

And nightly under the simple stars
As I rode to sleep the owls were bearing the farm away,
All the moon long I heard, blessed among stables, the nightjars 25
   Flying with the ricks, and the horses
      Flashing into the dark.

And then to awake, and the farm, like a wanderer white
With the dew, come back, the cock on his shoulder: it was all
   Shining, it was Adam and maiden, 30
      The sky gathered again
   And the sun grew round that very day.
So it must have been after the birth of the simple light
In the first, spinning place, the spellbound horses walking warm
   Out of the whinnying green stable 35
      On to the fields of praise.

And honoured among foxes and pheasants by the gay house
Under the new made clouds and happy as the heart was long,
   In the sun born over and over,
      I ran my heedless ways, 40
   My wishes raced through the house-high hay
And nothing I cared, at my sky blue trades, that time allows
In all his tuneful turning so few and such morning songs
   Before the children green and golden
      Follow him out of grace. 45

Nothing I cared, in the lamb white days, that time would take me
Up to the swallow thronged loft by the shadow of my hand,
   In the moon that is always rising,
      Nor that riding to sleep
   I should hear him fly with the high fields 50
And wake to the farm forever fled from the childless land.
Oh as I was young and easy in the mercy of his means,
      Time held me green and dying
      Though I sang in my chains like the sea.

Richard Cory

Edwin Arlington Robinson (1869–1935)

Whenever Richard Cory went down town,
We people on the pavement looked at him:
He was a gentleman from sole to crown,
Clean favored and imperially slim.

And he was always quietly arrayed,   5
And he was always human when he talked;
But still he fluttered pulses when he said,
"Good-morning," and he glittered when he walked.

And he was rich—yes, richer than a king—
And admirably schooled in every grace: 10
In fine, we thought that he was everything
To make us wish that we were in his place.

So on we worked, and waited for the light,
And went without the meat and cursed the bread;
And Richard Cory, one calm summer night,   15
Went home and put a bullet through his head.

Spring and Fall: To a Young Child

Gerard Manley Hopkins (1884–1889)

Márgarét, áre you gríeving
Over Goldengrove unleaving?
Leáves, líke the things of man, you
With your fresh thoughts care for, can you?
Áh! ás the heart grows older   5
It will come to such sights colder
By and by, nor spare a sigh
Though worlds of wanwood leafmeal lie.
And yet you will weep and know why.
Now no matter, child, the name: 10
Sórrow's springs áre the same.

"Richard Cory" reprinted by permission of Charles Scribner's Sons from *The Children of the Night* by Edwin Arlington Robinson (1897).

34

Nor mouth had, no nor mind expressed
What heart heard of, ghost guessed:
It ís the blight man was born for,
It is Margaret you mourn for.   15

She Walks in Beauty

George Gordon, Lord Byron (1788–1824)

She walks in Beauty, like the night
    Of cloudless climes and starry skies;
And all that's best of dark and bright
    Meet in her aspect and her eyes:
Thus mellowed to that tender light   5
    Which Heaven to gaudy day denies.

One shade the more, one ray the less,
    Had half impaired the nameless grace
Which waves in every raven tress,
    Or softly lightens o'er her face;   10
Where thoughts serenely sweet express,
    How pure, how dear their dwelling-place.

And on that cheek, and o'er that brow,
    So soft, so calm, yet eloquent,
The smiles that win, the tints that glow,   15
    But tell of days in goodness spent,
A mind at peace with all below,
    A heart whose love is innocent!

i sing of Olaf glad and big

e. e. cummings (1894–1962)

i sing of Olaf glad and big
whose warmest heart recoiled at war:
a conscientious object-or

his wellbeloved colonel(trig
westpointer most succinctly bred)   5
took erring Olaf soon in hand;

but—though an host of overjoyed
noncoms(first knocking on the head
him)do through icy waters roll
that helplessness which others stroke   10
with brushes recently employed
anent this muddy toiletbowl,
while kindred intellects evoke
allegiance per blunt instruments—
Olaf(being to all intents   15
a corpse and wanting any rag
upon what God unto him gave)
responds,without getting annoyed
"I will not kiss your f.ing flag"

straightway the silver bird looked grave   20
(departing hurriedly to shave)

but—though all kinds of officers
(a yearning nation's blueeyed pride)
their passive prey did kick and curse
until for wear their clarion   25
voices and boots were much the worse,
and egged the firstclassprivates on
his rectum wickedly to tease
by means of skilfully applied
bayonets roasted hot with heat—   30
Olaf(upon what were once knees)
does almost ceaselessly repeat
"there is some s. I will not eat"

our president,being of which
assertions duly notified   35
threw the yellowsonofabitch
into a dungeon,where he died

Christ(of His mercy infinite)
i pray to see;and Olaf,too

preponderatingly because   40
unless statistics lie he was
more brave than me:more blond than you.

To Phoebe

W. S. Gilbert (1836–1911)

"Gentle, modest little flower
   Sweet epitome of May
Love me but for half-an-hour,
   Love me, love me, little fay."
Sentences so fiercely flaming   5
   In your tiny shell-like ear,
I should always be exclaiming
   If I loved you, PHOEBE dear!

"Smiles that thrill from any distance
   Shed upon me while I sing!   10
Please ecstaticize existence,
   Love me, oh, thou fairy thing!"
Words like these, outpouring sadly,
   You'd perpetually hear,
If I loved you, fondly, madly; —   15
   But I do not, PHOEBE dear!

from An Essay on Criticism

Alexander Pope (1688–1744)

   But most by *Numbers* judge a Poet's song;
And smooth or rough, with them is right or wrong:
In the bright Muse, though thousand charms conspire,
Her voice is all these tuneful fools admire;
Who haunt Parnassus but to please their ear,   5
Not mend their minds; as some to Church repair,
Not for the doctrine, but the music there.
These equal syllables alone require,
Tho' oft the ear the open vowels tire;
While expletives their feeble aid do join;   10
And ten low words oft creep in one dull line:
While they ring round the same unvaried chimes,
With sure returns of still expected rhymes;
Where-e'er you find "the cooling western breeze,"
In the next line, it "whispers through the trees:"   15
If crystal streams "with pleasing murmurs creep,"
The reader's threatened (not in vain) with "sleep:"

;t and only couplet fraught
neaning thing they call a thought,
kandrine ends the song   20
unded snake, drags its slow length along.
Leave such to tune their own dull rhymes, and know
What's roundly smooth or languishingly slow;
And praise the easy vigour of a line,
Where Denham's strength, and Waller's sweetness join.   25
True ease in writing comes from art, not chance,
As those move easiest who have learned to dance.
'Tis not enough no harshness gives offence,
The sound must seem an Echo to the sense:
Soft is the strain when Zephyr gently blows,   30
And the smooth stream in smoother numbers flows;
But when loud surges lash the sounding shore,
The hoarse, rough verse should like the torrent roar:
When Ajax strives some rock's vast weight to throw,
The line too labours, and the words move slow;   35
Not so, when swift Camilla scours the plain,
Flies o'er the unbending corn, and skims along the main.
Hear how Timotheus' varied lays surprize,
And bid alternate passions fall and rise!

Numbers (l. 1): versification, especially rhythm.   *Denham and Waller* (l. 25):
seventeenth-century poets.   *Camilla* (l. 36): a swift-footed warrior maiden in Virgil's
Aeneid.   *Timotheus* (l. 38): a famous Greek musician.

Jabberwocky

Lewis Carroll (1832–1898)

'Twas brillig, and the slithy toves
    Did gyre and gimble in the wabe;
All mimsy were the borogoves,
    And the mome raths outgrabe.

"Beware the Jabberwock, my son!   5
    The jaws that bite, the claws that catch!
Beware the Jubjub bird, and shun
    The frumious Bandersnatch!"

He took his vorpal sword in hand
    Long time the manxome foe he sought —   10
So rested he by the Tumtum tree,
    And stood awhile in thought.

38

And, as in uffish thought he stood,
   The Jabberwock, with eyes of flame,
Came whiffling through the tulgey wood,   15
   And burbled as it came!

One, two! One, two! And through and through
   The vorpal blade went snicker-snack!
He left it dead, and with its head
   He went galumphing back.   20

"And hast thou slain the Jabberwock?
   Come to my arms, my beamish boy!
O frabjous day! Callooh! Callay!"
   He chortled in his joy.

'Twas brillig, and the slithy toves   25
   Did gyre and gimble in the wabe;
All mimsy were the borogoves,
   And the mome raths outgrabe.

Three

The Strategies of Poetry

As you have seen in reading the poems in Chapter One, poets themselves do not agree on what poetry is, how it is created, or what function it serves. For Auden, "poetry makes nothing happen," while Marianne Moore asserts that poems can be useful; Shakespeare declares that his poetry will confer immortality on his beloved, and MacLeish brands this a boastful lie. In Chapter Two, we have considered how poets use individual words.

Although beginning with the smallest unit of the poem, the word, has obvious advantages, you no doubt quickly discovered that the meaning of an individual word is often determined by other things in the poem. The full meaning of key words in the final stanza of Masefield's "Cargoes" ("Dirty" and "cheap," for example; p. 29) emerges from their contrast with the romantic and exotic words of the preceding stanzas.

Before we turn to other characteristics of poetry, it is worth reminding ourselves that all of us — poets and readers of poetry — are users of language. When we struggle with a speech or an essay, we are engaging in the same struggle as the poet. Our language is replete with synonyms, and every time we stop to ponder (think? meditate on? consider? deliberate on?) which word is most appropriate, we are doing what the poet does.

The same can be said about the strategies of poetry. Try to describe to someone your emotional state and the chances are that you will quickly reach for a comparison introduced by "like" or "as." You will understand perfectly well what someone means if he tells you that the college is a factory or that the office he works in is a snakepit. Nor will you have trouble when someone tells you he is reading Shakespeare or that he was so scared his hair stood on end. We may not realize, or even care to realize, that when we speak in this manner we are using simile, metaphor, metonymy, or hyperbole. But we are, and for the poet these are some of the most common and important devices of language.

In studying these devices, we move from the small unit, the word, to the larger unit of the phrase, and thence to the clause and the entire poem; each device may operate at any of these levels and it is thus important to recognize the different devices. But recognizing them is only the first step. It is far more important that you understand the way in which the devices work in a poem, how they have made it possible for the poet to say what he wants to say. One way of getting at this understanding is to consider why in some of the poems that employ simile as the major device, Joseph Campbell's "The Old Woman" (p. 43) and Christina Rossetti's "A Birthday" (p. 44), for example, we have a series of different similes bound together by a common attitude or feeling; whereas in others, Wilbur's "A Simile for Her Smile" (p. 43) and Frost's "The Silken Tent" (p. 46), the entire poem is the complex working out of a single simile. Or you might find it illuminating to compare Tichbourne's "Elegy — Written . . . before His Execution" (p. 63) and Pearse's "Last Lines" (p. 59), both written under the same dramatic circumstances, in terms of the poetic devices each poem employs.

A final word. Poems are written for many reasons, but one of them is surely not so that they can be neatly fitted into anthologies to demonstrate this, that, or the other theory or category. Many of the poems that follow rely heavily or exclusively on a single device; others employ a number of devices. Tichbourne's poem might just as easily have been placed under metaphor, for the entire first stanza is a series of metaphors. It has been included under paradox because that is the device governing the second and final stanzas. And there is an additional reason. If you examine the metaphors of the opening stanza, you will discover that they embody paradoxes. Not only do the poems not fit neatly into categories, the categories themselves are often inadequate. The point is that learning to recognize these devices provides us with a way into the poem's meaning and a vocabulary for discussing it, but we must constantly keep in mind that the complexities of poetic language are far richer and subtler than the analytic language we use to describe them.

Simile

A Simile for Her Smile

Richard Wilbur (1921–   )

Your smiling, or the hope, the thought of it,
Makes in my mind such pause and abrupt ease
As when the highway bridgegates fall,
Balking the hasty traffic, which must sit
On each side massed and staring, while   5
Deliberately the drawbridge starts to rise:

Then horns are hushed, the oilsmoke rarefies,
Above the idling motors one can tell
The packet's smooth approach, the slip,
Slip of the silken river past the sides,   10
The ringing of clear bells, the dip
And slow cascading of the paddle wheel.

The Old Woman

Joseph Campbell (1879–1944)

As a white candle
In a holy place,
So is the beauty
Of an agèd face.

As the spent radiance   5
Of the winter sun,
So is a woman
With her travail done.

Her brood gone from her,
And her thoughts are still   10
As the waters
Under a ruined mill.

As Birds Are Fitted to the Boughs

Louis Simpson (1923–   )

As birds are fitted to the boughs
That blossom on the tree
And whisper when the south wind blows —
So was my love to me.

And still she blossoms in my mind   5
And whispers softly, though
The clouds are fitted to the wind,
The wind is to the snow.

A Birthday

Christina Rossetti (1830–1894)

My heart is like a singing bird
    Whose nest is in a watered shoot;
My heart is like an apple-tree
    Whose boughs are bent with thick-set fruit;
My heart is like a rainbow shell   5
    That paddles in a halcyon sea;
My heart is gladder than all these,
    Because my love is come to me.

Raise me a dais of silk and down;
    Hang it with vair and purple dyes;   10
Carve it in doves and pomegranates,
    And peacocks with a hundred eyes;
Work it in gold and silver grapes,
    In leaves and silver fleurs-de-lys;
Because the birthday of my life   15
    Is come, my love is come to me.

"As Birds Are Fitted to the Boughs," copyright 1955 by Louis Simpson. Reprinted with the permission of Charles Scribner's Sons from *Good News of Death and Other Poems* by Louis Simpson. (*Poets of Today II.*)

44

To Daffodils

Robert Herrick (1591–1674)

Fair daffodils, we weep to see
  You haste away so soon;
As yet the early-rising sun
  Has not attained his noon.
    Stay, stay,   5
  Until the hasting day
    Has run
  But to the evensong;
And, having prayed together, we
  Will go with you along.   10

We have short time to stay as you;
  We have as short a spring;
As quick a growth to meet decay
  As you, or anything.
    We die   15
  As your hours do, and dry
    Away
  Like to the summer's rain;
Or as the pearls of morning's dew
  Ne'er to be found again.   20

Sic Vita

Henry King (1592–1669)

Like to the falling of a star,
Or as the flights of eagles are,
Or like the fresh spring's gaudy hue,
Or silver drops of morning dew,
Or like a wind that chafes the flood,   5
Or bubbles which on water stood:
Even such is man, whose borrowed light
Is straight called in, and paid to night.
  The wind blows out, the bubble dies;
  The spring entombed in autumn lies;   10
  The dew dries up, the star is shot;
  The flight is past, and man forgot.

A Red, Red Rose

Robert Burns (1759–1796)

O, my luve is like a red red rose
   That's newly sprung in June:
O, my luve is like the melodie
   That's sweetly played in tune.

As fair art thou, my bonnie lass,   5
   So deep in luve am I;
And I will luve thee still, my dear,
   Till a' the seas gang dry.

Till a' the seas gang dry, my dear,
   And the rocks melt wi' the sun;   10
And I will luve thee still, my dear
   While the sands o' life shall run.

And fare thee weel, my only luve!
   And fare thee weel a while!
And I will come again, my luve,   15
   Tho' it were ten thousand mile.

The Silken Tent

Robert Frost (1874–1963)

She is as in a field a silken tent
At midday when a sunny summer breeze
Has dried the dew and all its ropes relent,
So that in guys it gently sways at ease,
And its supporting central cedar pole,   5
That is its pinnacle to heavenward
And signifies the sureness of the soul,

Seems to owe naught to any single cord,
But strictly held by none, is loosely bound
By countless silken ties of love and thought 10
To everything on earth the compass round,
And only by one's going slightly taut
In the capriciousness of summer air
Is of the slightest bondage made aware.

Metaphor and Personification

Martin Luther King, Jr.

Gwendolyn Brooks (1915–   )

A man went forth with gifts.

He was a prose poem.
He was a tragic grace.
He was a warm music.

He tried to heal the vivid volcanoes. 5
His ashes are
    reading the world.

His Dream still wishes to anoint
    the barricades of faith and of control.

His word still burns the center of the sun, 10
    above the thousands and the
    hundred thousands.

The word was Justice. It was spoken.

So it shall be spoken.
So it shall be done. 15

Shine, Perishing Republic

Robinson Jeffers (1887–1962)

While this America settles in the mold of its vulgarity,
    heavily thickening to empire,
And protest, only a bubble in the molten mass, pops and sighs out,
    and the mass hardens,

I sadly smiling remember that the flower fades to make fruit, the
    fruit rots to make earth.
Out of the mother; and through the spring exultances, ripeness and
    decadence; and home to the mother.

You making haste haste on decay: not blameworthy; life is good, be
    it stubbornly long or suddenly   5
A mortal splendor: meteors are not needed less than mountains:
    shine, perishing republic.

But for my children, I would have them keep their distance from
    the thickening center; corruption
Never has been compulsory, when the cities lie at the monster's feet
    there are left the mountains.

And boys, be in nothing so moderate as in love of man, a clever
    servant, insufferable master.
There is the trap that catches noblest spirits, that caught — they say — God,
    when he walked on earth.   10

As I Walked Out One Evening

W. H. Auden (1907–   )

As I walked out one evening,
  Walking down Bristol Street,
The crowds upon the pavement
  Were fields of harvest wheat.

And down by the brimming river
  I heard a lover sing
Under an arch of the railway:
  "Love has no ending.

"I'll love you dear, I'll love you
  Till China and Africa meet,
And the river jumps over the mountain
  And the salmon sing in the street.

"I'll love you till the ocean
  Is folded and hung up to dry,
And the seven stars go squawking
  Like geese about the sky.

The years shall run like rabbits,
  For in my arms I hold
The Flower of the Ages,
  And the first love of the world."

But all the clocks in the city
  Began to whirr and chime:
"O let not Time deceive you,
  You cannot conquer Time.

"In the burrows of the Nightmare
  Where Justice naked is,
Time watches from the shadow
  And coughs when you would kiss.

"In headaches and in worry
  Vaguely life leaks away,
And Time will have his fancy
  Tomorrow or to-day.

"Into many a green valley
  Drifts the appalling snow;
Time breaks the threaded dances
  And the diver's brilliant bow.

"O plunge your hands in water,
  Plunge them in up to the wrist;
Stare, stare in the basin
  And wonder what you've missed.

5

10

15

20

25

30

35

40

"The glacier knocks in the cupboard,
   The desert sighs in the bed,
And the crack in the tea-cup opens
   A lane to the land of the dead.

"Where the beggars raffle the banknotes   45
   And the Giant is enchanting to Jack,
And the Lily-white Boy is a Roarer,
   And Jill goes down on her back.

"O look, look in the mirror,
   O look in your distress;   50
Life remains a blessing
   Although you cannot bless.

"O stand, stand at the window
   As the tears scald and start;
You shall love your crooked neighbor   55
   With your crooked heart."

It was late, late in the evening,
   The lovers they were gone;
The clocks had ceased their chiming,
   And the deep river ran on.   60

seven stars (l. 15): The Pleiades.   Roarer (l. 47): a reveller

To His Coy Mistress

Andrew Marvell (1621–1678)

Had we but world enough, and time,
This coyness, lady, were no crime.
We would sit down, and think which way
To walk, and pass our long love's day.
Thou by the Indian Ganges' side   5
Shouldst rubies find; I by the tide
Of Humber would complain. I would
Love you ten years before the flood,
And you should, if you please, refuse
Till the conversion of the Jews.   10
My vegetable love should grow
Vaster than empires, and more slow.

An hundred years should go to praise
Thine eyes, and on thy forehead gaze.
Two hundred to adore each breast,   15
But thirty thousand to the rest.
An age at least to every part,
And the last age should show your heart.
For, lady, you deserve this state,
Nor would I love at lower rate.   20
   But at my back I always hear
Time's winged chariot hurrying near;
And yonder all before us lie
Deserts of vast eternity.
Thy beauty shall no more be found;   25
Nor, in thy marble vault, shall sound
My echoing song; then worms shall try
That long-preserved virginity;
And your quaint honor turn to dust,
And into ashes all my lust.   30
The grave's a fine and private place,
But none, I think, do there embrace.
   Now therefore, while the youthful hue
Sits on thy skin like morning dew,
And while thy willing soul transpires   35
At every pore with instant fires,
Now let us sport us while we may;
And now, like amorous birds of prey,
Rather at once our time devour,
Than languish in his slow-chapped power.   40
Let us roll all our strength, and all
Our sweetness, up into one ball;
And tear our pleasures with rough strife,
Thorough the iron gates of life.
Thus, though we cannot make our sun   45
Stand still, yet we will make him run.

A Valediction: Forbidding Mourning

John Donne (1572–1631)

As virtuous men pass mildly away,
   And whisper to their souls, to go,
Whilst some of their sad friends do say,
   The breath goes now, and some say, No;

51

So let us melt, and make no noise,
    No tear-floods, nor sigh-tempests move,
'Twere profanation of our joys
    To tell the laity our love.

Moving of th' earth brings harms and fears,
    Men reckon what it did and meant,
But trepidation of the spheres,
    Though greater far, is innocent.

Dull sublunary lovers' love
    (Whose soul is sense) cannot admit
Absence, because it doth remove
    Those things which elemented it.

But we by a love, so much refined,
    That our selves know not what it is,
Inter-assuréd of the mind,
    Care less, eyes, lips, and hands to miss.

Our two souls therefore, which are one,
    Though I must go, endure not yet
A breach, but an expansion,
    Like gold to airy thinness beat.

If they be two, they are two so
    As stiff twin compasses are two;
Thy soul the fixed foot makes no show
    To move, but doth, if the other do.

And though it in the center sit,
    Yet when the other far doth roam,
It leans, and hearkens after it,
    And grows erect, as that comes home.

Such wilt thou be to me, who must
    Like th' other foot, obliquely run;
Thy firmness makes my circle just,
    And makes me end, where I begun.

["Hope" is the thing with feathers]

Emily Dickinson (1830–1886)

"Hope" is the thing with feathers —
That perches in the soul —
And sings the tune without the words —
And never stops — at all —

And sweetest — in the Gale — is heard —   5
And sore must be the storm —
That could abash the little Bird
That kept so many warm —

I've heard it in the chillest land —
And on the strangest Sea —   10
Yet, never, in Extremity,
It asked a crumb — of Me.

[Hope is a strange invention]

Emily Dickinson (1830–1886)

Hope is a strange invention —
A Patent of the Heart —
In unremitting action
Yet never wearing out —

Of this electric Adjunct   5
Not anything is known
But it's unique momentum
Embellish all we own —

[Hope is a subtle Glutton]

Emily Dickinson (1830–1886)

Hope is a subtle Glutton —
He feeds upon the Fair —
And yet — inspected closely
What Abstinence is there —

His is the Halcyon Table — 5
That never seats but One —
And whatsoever is consumed
The same amount remain —

On First Looking into Chapman's Homer

John Keats (1795–1821)

Much have I traveled in the realms of gold,
And many goodly states and kingdoms seen;
Round many western islands have I been
Which bards in fealty to Apollo hold.
Oft of one wide expanse had I been told 5
That deep-browed Homer ruled as his demesne;
Yet did I never breathe its pure serene
Till I heard Chapman speak out loud and bold:
Then felt I like some watcher of the skies
When a new planet swims into his ken; 10
Or like stout Cortez when with eagle eyes
He stared at the Pacific — and all his men
Looked at each other with a wild surmise —
Silent, upon a peak in Darien.

title: George Chapman, Elizabethan poet and translator of Homer.   *Cortez* (l.11): Balboa, not Cortez, first saw the Pacific from the mountains of Darien in Panama.

Symbol and Allegory

[Apparently with no surprise]

Emily Dickinson (1830–1886)

Apparently with no surprise
To any happy Flower
The Frost beheads it at its play —
In accidental power —
The blond assassin passes on —   5
The Sun proceeds unmoved
To measure off another Day
For an approving God.

Design

Robert Frost (1874–1963)

I found a dimpled spider, fat and white,
On a white heal-all, holding up a moth
Like a white piece of rigid satin cloth —
Assorted characters of death and blight
Mixed ready to begin the morning right,   5
Like the ingredients of a witches' broth
A snow-drop spider, a flower like froth,
And dead wings carried like a paper kite.

What had that flower to do with being white,
The wayside blue and innocent heal-all?   10
What brought the kindred spider to that height,
Then steered the white moth thither in the night?
What but design of darkness to appall? —
If design govern in a thing so small.

Loveliest of Trees

A. E. Housman (1859–1936)

Loveliest of trees, the cherry now
Is hung with bloom along the bough,
And stands about the woodland ride
Wearing white for Eastertide.

Now of my threescore years and ten,   5
Twenty will not come again,
And take from seventy springs a score,
It only leaves me fifty more.

And since to look at things in bloom
Fifty springs are little room,   10
About the woodlands I will go
To see the cherry hung with snow.

The Silver Penny

Walter de la Mare (1867–1900)

"Sailorman, I'll give to you
    My bright silver penny,
If out to sea you'll sail me
    And my dear sister Jenny."

"Get in, young sir, I'll sail ye   5
    And your dear sister Jenny,
But pay she shall her golden locks
    Instead of your penny."

They sail away, they sail away,
   O fierce the winds blew!   10
The foam flew in clouds,
   And dark the night grew!

And all the green sea-water
   Climbed steep into the boat;
Back to the shore again   15
   Sail they will not.

Drowned is the sailorman,
   Drowned is sweet Jenny,
And drowned in the deep sea
   A bright silver penny.   20

Sailing to Byzantium

W. B. Yeats (1865–1939)

That is no country for old men. The young
In one another's arms, birds in the trees
— Those dying generations — at their song,
The salmon-falls, the mackerel-crowded seas,
Fish, flesh, or fowl, commend all summer long   5
Whatever is begotten, born, and dies.
Caught in that sensual music all neglect
Monuments of unaging intellect.

An aged man is but a paltry thing,
A tattered coat upon a stick, unless   10
Soul clap its hands and sing, and louder sing
For every tatter in its mortal dress,
Nor is there singing school but studying
Monuments of its own magnificence;
And therefore I have sailed the seas and come   15
To the holy city of Byzantium.

O sages standing in God's holy fire
As in the gold mosaic of a wall,
Come from the holy fire, perne in a gyre,
And be the singing-masters of my soul.   20
Consume my heart away; sick with desire
And fastened to a dying animal
It knows not what it is; and gather me
Into the artifice of eternity.

Once out of nature I shall never take   25
My bodily form from any natural thing,
But such a form as Grecian goldsmiths make
Of hammered gold and gold enameling
To keep a drowsy Emperor awake;
Or set upon a golden bough to sing   30
To lords and ladies of Byzantium
Of what is past, or passing, or to come.

perne in a gyre (l. 19): whirl in a spiral motion.   *keep a drowsy Emperor awake* (l. 29):
"I have read somewhere," Yeats wrote, "that in the Emperor's palace at Byzantium was a
tree made of gold and silver, and artificial birds that sang."

I Have Longed to Move Away

Dylan Thomas (1914–1953)

I have longed to move away
From the hissing of the spent lie
And the old terrors' continual cry
Growing more terrible as the day
Goes over the hill into the deep sea;   5
I have longed to move away
From the repetition of salutes,
For there are ghosts in the air
And ghostly echoes on paper,
And the thunder of calls and notes.   10

I have longed to move away but am afraid;
Some life, yet unspent, might explode
Out of the old lie burning on the ground,
And, crackling into the air, leave me half-blind.
Neither by night's ancient fear,   15
The parting of hat from hair,
Pursed lips at the receiver,
Shall I fall to death's feather.
By these I would not care to die,
Half convention and half lie.   20

Last Lines — 1916

Padraic Pearse (1879–1916)

(Written the night before his execution)

The beauty of the world hath made me sad,
This beauty that will pass;
Sometimes my heart hath shaken with great joy
To see a leaping squirrel in a tree,
Or a red lady-bird upon a stalk,   5
Or little rabbits in a field at evening,
Lit by a slanting sun,
Or some green hill where shadows drifted by,
Some quiet hill where mountainy man hath sown
And soon would reap; near to the gate of Heaven;   10
Or children with bare feet upon the sands
Of some ebbed sea, or playing on the streets
Of little towns in Connacht,
Things young and happy.
And then my heart hath told me: 15
These will pass,
Will pass and change, will die and be no more,
Things bright and green, things young and happy;
And I have gone upon my way
Sorrowful.   20

The Ballad of Bigger Thomas

E. Curmie Price (1940–   )

Bigger than your doubt, Thomas,
the sensible world beats its head
against city streets, trying
to make sense of your existential act.

Now that we're talking debts,   5
let's admit it; Camus' Meursault
owes something to Wright's Thomas,
who taught them *all* the exaltation
of violence in a contingent world.

Oh yes, yes; I've heard of Sartre,   10
Genet, and the absurd; just yesterday,
however, lost in *Native Son,* I had put
my fist through a gray world before I knew it.

Call it instinct, mammoth expectations.
Bigger Thomas rides again along   15
the tributes of my thoughts.

title: Bigger Thomas is the hero of Richard Wright's novel *Native Son*. Like Meursault, the
hero of Albert Camus' novel *The Stranger,* Bigger discovers meaning in his life as a result
of committing a murder.   *Sartre* (l. 10) and *Genet* (l. 11): Jean-Paul Sartre and Jean Genet,
contemporary French existentialists.

Symbols

John Drinkwater (1882–1937)

I saw in a poet's song,
In a river-reach and a gallows-hill,
In a bridal bed, and a secret wrong,
In a crown of thorns: in a daffodil.

60

I imagined measureless time in a day,   5
And starry space in a waggon-road,
And the treasure of all good harvests lay
In the single seed that the sower sowed.

My garden-wind had driven and havened again
All ships that ever had gone to sea,   10
And I saw the glory of all dead men
In the shadow that went by the side of men.

Ode

William Collins (1721–1759)

How sleep the brave, who sink to rest,
By all their country's wishes blest!
When Spring, with dewy fingers cold,
Returns to deck their hallowed mold,
She there shall dress a sweeter sod,   5
Than Fancy's feet have ever trod.

By fairy hands their knell is rung,
By forms unseen their dirge is sung;
There Honour comes, a pilgrim grey,
To bless the turf that wraps their clay,   10
And Freedom shall awhile repair,
To dwell a weeping hermit there!

To Autumn

John Keats (1795–1821)

Season of mists and mellow fruitfulness,
    Close bosom-friend of the maturing sun;
Conspiring with him how to load and bless
    With fruit the vines that round the thatch-eves run;
To bend with apples the moss'd cottage-trees,   5
    And fill all fruit with ripeness to the core;
        To swell the gourd, and plump the hazel shells
With a sweet kernel; to set budding more,
    And still more, later flowers for the bees,
    Until they think warm days will never cease,   10
        For Summer has o'er-brimm'd their clammy cells.

Who hath not seen thee oft amid thy store?
　　Sometimes whoever seeks abroad may find
Thee sitting careless on a granary floor,
　　Thy hair soft-lifted by the winnowing wind;　　　　　　　15
Or on a half-reap'd furrow sound asleep,
　　Drows'd with the fume of poppies, while thy hook
　　　Spares the next swath and all its twined flowers:
And sometimes like a gleaner thou dost keep
　　Steady thy laden head across a brook;　　　　　　　　　20
　　Or by a cyder-press, with patient look,
　　　Thou watchest the last oozings hours by hours.

Where are the songs of Spring? Ay, where are they?
　　Think not of them, thou hast thy music too, —
While barred clouds bloom the soft-dying day,　　　　　　25
　　And touch the stubble-plains with rosy hue;
Then in a wailful choir the small gnats mourn
　　Among the river sallows, borne aloft
　　　Or sinking as the light wind lives or dies;
And full-grown lambs loud bleat from hilly bourn;　　　　30
　　Hedge-crickets sing; and now with treble soft
The red-breast whistles from a garden-croft;
　　And gathering swallows twitter in the skies.

The Garden of Love

William Blake (1757–1827)

I went to the Garden of Love
And saw what I never had seen:
A Chapel was built in the midst,
Where I used to play on the green.

And the gates of this Chapel were shut,　　　　　　　　　5
And "Thou shalt not" writ over the door;
So I turned to the Garden of Love
That so many sweet flowers bore;

And I saw it was filled with graves,
And tombstones where flowers should be;　　　　　　　　10
And priests in black gowns were walking their rounds,
And binding with briars my joys and desires.

Paradox

On a Squirrel Crossing the Road
in Autumn, in New England

Richard Eberhart (1904–   )

It is what he does not know,
Crossing the road under the elm trees,
About the mechanism of my car,
About the Commonwealth of Massachusetts,
About Mozart, India, Arcturus,   5

That wins my praise. I engage
At once in whirling squirrel-praise.

He obeys the orders of nature
Without knowing them.
It is what he does not know   10
That makes him beautiful.
Such a knot of little purposeful nature!

I who can see him as he cannot see himself
Repose in the ignorance that is his blessing.

It is what man does not know of God   15
Composes the visible poem of the world.
                    . . . Just missed him!

Elegy, Written with His Own Hand
in the Tower before His Execution

Chidiock Tichborne (1558?–1586)

My prime of youth is but a frost of cares,
   My feast of joy is but a dish of pain,
My crop of corn is but a field of tares,
   And all my good is but vain hope of gain:
The day is past, and yet I saw no sun,   5
And now I live, and now my life is done.

My tale was heard, and yet it was not told,
　My fruit is fall'n, and yet my leaves are green,
My youth is spent, and yet I am not old,
　I saw the world, and yet I was not seen:　　　　　　　10
My thread is cut, and yet it is not spun,
And now I live, and now my life is done.

I sought my death, and found it in my womb,
　I looked for life, and saw it was a shade,
I trod the earth, and knew it was my tomb,　　　　　　15
　And now I die, and now I was but made:
My glass is full, and now my glass is run,
And now I live, and now my life is done.

Brahma

Ralph Waldo Emerson (1803–1882)

If the red slayer think he slays,
　Of if the slain think he is slain,
They know not well the subtle ways
　I keep, and pass, and turn again.

Far or forgot to me is near;　　　　　　　　　　　　5
　Shadow and sunlight are the same;
The vanished gods to me appear;
　And one to me are shame and fame.

They reckon ill who leave me out;
　When me they fly, I am the wings;　　　　　　　　10
I am the doubter and the doubt,
　And I the hymn the Brahmin sings.

The strong gods pine for my abode,
　And pine in vain the sacred Seven;
But thou, meek lover of the good!　　　　　　　　　15
　Find me, and turn thy back on heaven.

Eternity

William Blake (1757–1827)

He who binds himself to a joy
Does the wingèd life destroy;
But he who kisses the joy as it flies
Lives in eternity's sun rise.

The Liar

LeRoi Jones (1934–   )

What I thought was love
in me, I find a thousand instances
as fear. (Of the tree's shadow
winding around the chair, a distant music
of frozen birds rattling   5
in the cold.)
                    Where ever I go to claim
my flesh, there are entrances
of spirit. And even its comforts
are hideous uses I strain
to understand.
                    Though I am a man   10
who is loud
on the birth
of his ways. Publicly redefining
each change in my soul, as if I had predicted
them,
          and profited, biblically, even tho   15
          their chanting weight,
                              erased familiarity
                              from my face.
                              A question I think,
an answer; whatever sits
counting the minutes
till you die.   20

            When they say, "It is Roi
            who is dead?" I wonder
            who will they mean?

65

Paradox

Vassar Miller (1924–   )

Mild yoke of Christ, most harsh to me not bearing,
You bruise the neck that balks, the hands that break you;
Sweet bread and wine, bitter to me not sharing,
You scar and scorch the throat that will not take you;
Mount where He taught, you cripple feet not bloody   5
From your sharp flints of eight-fold benediction;
Bright cross, most shameful stripped of the stripped body,
You crucify me safe from crucifixion:
Yet I, who am my own dilemma, jolting
My mind with thought lest it unthink its stiffness,   10
Rise to revolt against my own revolting.
Blind me to blindness, deafen me to deafness.
So will Your gifts of sight and hearing plunder
My eyes with lightning and my ears with thunder.

[Batter my heart, three-personed God]

John Donne (1572–1631)

Batter my heart, three-personed God, for You
As yet but knock, breathe, shine, and seek to mend.
That I may rise and stand, o'erthrow me, and bend
Your force to break, blow, burn, and make me new.
I, like an usurped town to another due,   5
Labor to admit You, but Oh! to no end.
Reason, Your viceroy in me, me should defend,
But is captived, and proves weak or untrue.
Yet dearly I love You, and would be lovèd fain,
But am betrothed unto Your enemy;   10
Divorce me, untie or break that knot again;
Take me to You, imprison me, for I,
Except You enthrall me, never shall be free,
Nor ever chaste, except You ravish me.

three-personed God (l. 1): Father, Son, and Holy Ghost of the Christian Trinity

"Paradox" reprinted from *Wage War on Silence* by Vassar Miller, by permission of Wesleyan University Press.

[Doing, a filthy pleasure is, and short]

Ben Jonson (1573–1637)

Doing, a filthy pleasure is, and short;
And done, we straight repent us of the sport:
Let us not then rush blindly unto it,
Like lustful beasts, they only know to do it:
For lust will languish, and that heat decay,   5
But thus, thus, keeping endless Holy-day,
Let us together closely lie, and kiss,
There is no labor, nor no shame in this;
This hath pleased, doth please, and long will please; never
Can this decay, but is beginning ever.   10

Irony

The Man He Killed

Thomas Hardy (1840–1928)

'Had he and I but met
    By some old ancient inn,
We should have sat us down to wet
    Right many a nipperkin!

'But ranged as infantry,   5
    And staring face to face,
I shot at him as he at me,
    And killed him in his place.

'I shot him dead because —
    Because he was my foe,   10
Just so: my foe of course he was;
    That's clear enough; although

"The Man He Killed" reprinted from *Collected Poems of Thomas Hardy* by permission of The Macmillan Company, the Hardy Estate, Macmillan London & Basingstoke, and The Macmillan Company of Canada Limited.

67

'He thought he'd 'list, perhaps,
  Off-hand like — just as I —
Was out of work — had sold his traps —   15
  No other reason why.

'Yes; quaint and curious war is!
  You shoot a fellow down
You'd treat if met where any bar is,
  Or help to half-a-crown.'   20

nipperkin (l. 4): a half-pint vessel for liquor

My Last Duchess

Ferrara

Robert Browning (1812–1889)

That's my last Duchess painted on the wall,
Looking as if she were alive. I call
That piece a wonder, now; Fra Pandolf's hands
Worked busily a day, and there she stands.
Will't please you sit and look at her? I said   5
"Fra Pandolf" by design, for never read
Strangers like you that pictured countenance,
The depth and passion of its earnest glance,
But to myself they turned (since none puts by
The curtain I have drawn for you, but I)   10
And seemed as they would ask me, if they durst,
How such a glance came there; so, not the first
Are you to turn and ask thus. Sir, 'twas not
Her husband's presence only, called that spot
Of joy into the Duchess' cheek; perhaps   15
Fra Pandolf chanced to say, "Her mantle laps
Over my lady's wrist too much," or, "Paint
Must never hope to reproduce the faint
Half-flush that dies along her throat." Such stuff
Was courtesy, she thought, and cause enough   20
For calling up that spot of joy. She had
A heart — how shall I say? — too soon made glad,
Too easily impressed; she liked whate'er
She looked on, and her looks went everywhere.

Ferrara: A city in Italy (near Venice) which flourished during the Italian Renaissance of the
fourteenth and fifteenth centuries.

Sir, 'twas all one! My favor at her breast,   25
The dropping of the daylight in the West,
The bough of cherries some officious fool
Broke in the orchard for her, the white mule
She rode with round the terrace—all and each
Would draw from her alike the approving speech,   30
Or blush, at least. She thanked men—good! but thanked
Somehow—I know not how—as if she ranked
My gift of a nine-hundred-years-old name
With anybody's gift. Who'd stoop to blame
This sort of trifling? Even had you skill   35
In speech—which I have not—to make your will
Quite clear to such an one, and say, "Just this
Or that in you disgusts me; here you miss,
Or there exceed the mark"—and if she let
Herself be lessoned so, nor plainly set   40
Her wits to yours, forsooth, and made excuse—
E'en then would be some stooping; and I choose
Never to stoop. Oh, sir, she smiled, no doubt,
Whene'er I passed her; but who passed without
Much the same smile? This grew; I gave commands;   45
Then all smiles stopped together. There she stands
As if alive. Will't please you rise? We'll meet
The company below, then. I repeat,
The Count your master's known munificence
Is ample warrant that no just pretense   50
Of mine for dowry will be disallowed;
Though his fair daughter's self, as I avowed
At starting, is my object. Nay, we'll go
Together down, sir. Notice Neptune, though,
Taming a sea-horse, thought a rarity,   55
Which Claus of Innsbruck cast in bronze for me!

War Is Kind

Stephen Crane (1871–1900)

Do not weep, maiden, for war is kind.
Because your lover threw wild hands toward the sky
And the affrighted steed ran on alone,
Do not weep.
War is kind.   5

Hoarse, booming drums of the regiment,
Little souls who thirst for fight,
These men were born to drill and die.
The unexplained glory flies above them,
Great is the battle-god, great, and his kingdom — 10
A field where a thousand corpses lie.

Do not weep, babe, for war is kind.
Because your father tumbled in the yellow trenches,
Raged at his breast, gulped and died,
Do not weep. 15
War is kind.

Swift blazing flag of the regiment,
Eagle with crest of red and gold,
These men were born to drill and die.
Point for them the virtue of slaughter, 20
Make plain to them the excellence of killing
And a field where a thousand corpses lie.
Mother whose heart hung humble as a button
On the bright splendid shroud of your son,
Do not weep. 25
War is kind.

For a Lady I Know

Countee Cullen (1903–1946)

She even thinks that up in heaven
Her class lies late and snores,
While poor black cherubs rise at seven
To do celestial chores.

Southern Cop

Sterling A. Brown (1901–   )

Let us forgive Ty Kendricks
The place was Darktown. He was young.
His nerves were jittery. The day was hot.
The Negro ran out of the alley.
And so Ty shot.   5

Let us understand Ty Kendricks
The Negro must have been dangerous,
Because he ran;
And here was a rookie with a chance
To prove himself man.   10

Let us condone Ty Kendricks
If we cannot decorate.
When he found what the Negro was running for,
It was all too late;
And all we can say for the Negro is   15
It was unfortunate.

Let us pity Ty Kendricks
He has been through enough,
Standing there, his big gun smoking,
Rabbit-scared, alone,   20
Having to hear the wenches wail
And the dying Negro moan.

"Southern Cop" reprinted by permission of Sterling A. Brown.

Four

Poems for Comparison and Evaluation

Looking back over his long and productive career as a poet, W. B. Yeats remarked toward the end of his life that many of his poems which seemed difficult or obscure would be better understood as the years went by and one poem lighted up another. Yeats was speaking with an awareness of the development and unity of his own works, of a relationship among his poems that his readers would gradually come to recognize and appreciate. The relationship of poems by different poets is of course another matter, but there is nonetheless a useful and fruitful sense in which a poem by one poet can light up the poem of another.

In considering the poems of earlier chapters, you have probably discovered a number of poems that were strikingly similar to one another, and you have probably found in their similarity an interesting and illuminating opportunity to compare and contrast them—even to better understand them. For example, comparisons between Emily Dickinson's ["Apparently with no surprise"] (p. 55) and Robert Frost's "Design" (p. 55), William Wordsworth's ["It is a beauteous evening"] and Phyllis McGinley's "Country Club Sunday," and Andrew Marvell's "To His Coy Mistress" and John Donne's "A Valediction: Forbidding Mourning" provide unique opportunities for insight and understanding. And a comparison of Dickinson's and Frost's poems might have led to a consideration of the way in which these two poets (and many others) invest a simple and ordinary natural occurrence with symbolic meaning. In discussing Phyllis McGinley's poem, you might have considered whether your appreciation of it was enhanced by Wordsworth's poem. A comparison of Marvell's and Donne's poems might very well have led to a consideration of the relationship between

73

poetry and belief—can we appreciate or respond to two poems that define love in such radically different ways?

In making comparisons you may have found that you were not only analyzing but evaluating and judging. As a matter of fact, it would be strange indeed if you had not been making evaluations and judgments from the very outset. Whether or not you were able at the outset to articulate your reasons, you undoubtedly decided you liked some poems and didn't like others. As you read and studied and discussed more poems, it is likely that your ability to understand and articulate your own responses to poems grew. This chapter brings together groups of poems that provide opportunities for comparisons ranging from similarity of theme and technique to differences in the symbolic treatment of the same objects. As you read the poems in each group, you will have no problem seeing the obvious relationships among them; more specific and detailed comparisons will depend on your analyses of the individual poems. In any case, they will provide you with the means of evaluating and judging and formulating general criteria about poetry that can be compared with those of your fellow students.

Evaluating and judging are not meant to suggest final, unalterable, or rigid procedures. If you turn back to some of the early poems in this volume, your response to them now—your evaluation and judgment—may differ markedly from your original response. Having read and analyzed many poems now, you may discover things about the earlier poems that you were unable to see originally. You have no doubt also had the experience of finding yourself baffled by a poem on first reading but discovering that as you worked at it you came to understand and even enjoy it. The understanding and enjoyment of poetry—or of particular poems—are not subject to some final mastery, like the multiplication tables. They are continuing and growing processes. Your evaluations and judgments of the poems in this chapter should be tempered by this realization. The poems in each group do not conceal some hierarchy of excellence that you are supposed to discover. The groupings have been made in order to focus on the process of judging and evaluating that avid readers of poetry continuously engage in, a process providing one more means of sharpening your critical and analytical abilities and thereby heightening your enjoyment of poetry. Enjoyment through understanding—that is what reading poetry is all about.

In a Station of the Metro

Ezra Pound (1885–   )

The apparition of these faces in the crowd;
Petals on a wet, black bough.

The Red Wheelbarrow

William Carlos Williams (1883–1963)

So much depends
upon
a red wheel
barrow
glazed with rain   5
water
beside the white
chickens.

"Out, Out—"

Robert Frost (1874–1963)

The buzz-saw snarled and rattled in the yard
And made dust and dropped stove-length sticks of wood,
Sweet-scented stuff when the breeze drew across it.
And from there those that lifted eyes could count
Five mountain ranges one behind the other   5
Under the sunset far into Vermont.
And the saw snarled and rattled, snarled and rattled,
As it ran light, or had to bear a load.
And nothing happened: day was all but done.
Call it a day, I wish they might have said   10
To please the boy by giving him the half hour
That a boy counts so much when saved from work.
His sister stood beside them in her apron
To tell them "Supper." At the word, the saw,
As if to prove saws knew what supper meant,   15
Leaped out at the boy's hand, or seemed to leap—
He must have given the hand. However it was,
Neither refused the meeting. But the hand!

The boy's first outcry was a rueful laugh,
As he swung toward them holding up the hand   20
Half in appeal, but half as if to keep
The life from spilling. Then the boy saw all—
Since he was old enough to know, big boy
Doing a man's work, though a child at heart—
He saw all spoiled. "Don't let him cut my hand off—   25
The doctor, when he comes. Don't let him, sister!"
So. But the hand was gone already.
The doctor put him in the dark of ether.
He lay and puffed his lips out with his breath.
And then—the watcher at his pulse took fright.   30
No one believed. They listened at his heart.
Little—less—nothing!—and that ended it.
No more to build on there. And they, since they
Were not the one dead, turned to their affairs.

title: taken from Macbeth's soliloquy on the death of Lady Macbeth (*Macbeth*, Act V, Scene 5)

Paul

James Wright (1927–   )

I used to see her in the door,
Lifting up her hand to wave
To citizens, or pass the hour
With neighboring wives who did not have
Anything more than time to say.   5

I used to see her in the door,
Simple and quiet woman, slim;
And hence, I think, Paul cared the more
The night they carried her from him,
The night they carried her away.   10

The doctor did not even ask
For any neighborly advice;
He knew he had a simple task,
And it was obvious from his eyes
There was not anything to say.   15

The doctor had a word for Paul;
He said that she was resting now,
And would not wake, and that was all.
And then he walked into the snow,
Into the snow he walked away.   20

And did Paul shriek and curse the air,
And did he pummel with his fist
Against the wall, or tear his hair
And rush outside to bite the mist
That did not have a thing to say?   25

He sat upon her ruffled bed,
And did not even look at me.
She was lovely, she was dead.
Some sparrows chirruped on a tree
Outside, and then they flew away.   30

On a Dying Boy

William Bell (1924–1948)

Oh leave his body broken on the rocks
where fainting sense may drown beneath the sound
of the complaining surf. His spirit mocks
our ignorant attempts to hem it round:
as eagerly as body sought the ground   5
into its native ocean must it flow.
Oh let his body lie where it was found,
there's nothing we can do to help him now.

And hide his face under his tattered coat
until the women come to where he lies,   10
they come to bind the silence in his throat
and shut the eternal darkness in his eyes,
to wash the cold sweat of his agonies
and wash the blood that's clotted on his brow.
Cover his face from the unfriendly skies,   15
there's nothing we can do to help him now.

"On a Dying Boy" from *Mountains Beneath Horizons* reprinted by permission of Faber
and Faber Ltd.

And watch even his enemies forget him,
the skies forget his sobs, the rocks his blood:
and think how neither rock nor sky dared let him
grow old enough for evil or for good;   20
and then forget him too. Even if we could
bring back the flower that's fallen from the bough,
bring back the flower that never left the bud,
there's nothing we can do to help him now.

[How the Waters closed above Him]

Emily Dickinson (1830–1886)

How the Waters closed above Him
We shall never know —
How He stretched His Anguish to us
That — is covered too —

Spreads the Pond Her Base of Lilies   5
Bold above the Boy
Whose unclaimed Hat and Jacket
Sum the History —

Elegy Written in a Country Churchyard

Thomas Gray (1716–1771)

The curfew tolls the knell of parting day,
   The lowing herd wind slowly o'er the lea,
The plowman homeward plods his weary way,
   And leaves the world to darkness and to me.

Now fades the glimmering landscape on the sight,   5
   And all the air a solemn stillness holds,
Save where the beetle wheels his droning flight,
   And drowsy tinklings lull the distant folds;

Save that from yonder ivy-mantled tower
    The moping owl does to the moon complain   10
Of such, as wandering near her secret bower,
    Molest her ancient solitary reign.

Beneath those rugged elms, that yew tree's shade,
    Where heaves the turf in many a moldering heap,
Each in his narrow cell forever laid,   15
    The rude forefathers of the hamlet sleep.

The breezy call of incense-breathing morn,
    The swallow twittering from the straw-built shed,
The cock's shrill clarion, or the echoing horn,
    No more shall rouse them from their lowly bed.   20

From them no more the blazing hearth shall burn,
    Or busy housewife ply her evening care;
No children run to lisp their sire's return,
    Or climb his knees the envied kiss to share.

Oft did the harvest to their sickle yield,   25
    Their furrow oft the stubborn glebe has broke;
How jocund did they drive their team afield!
    How bowed the woods beneath their sturdy stroke!

Let not Ambition mock their useful toil,
    Their homely joys, and destiny obscure;   30
Nor Grandeur hear with a disdainful smile
    The short and simple annals of the poor.

The boast of heraldry, the pomp of power,
    And all that beauty, all that wealth e'er gave,
Awaits alike the inevitable hour.   35
    The paths of glory lead but to the grave.

Nor you, ye proud, impute to these the fault,
    If Memory o'er their tomb no trophies raise,
Where through the long-drawn aisle and fretted vault
    The pealing anthem swells the note of praise.   40

Can storied urn or animated bust
    Back to its mansion call the fleeting breath?
Can Honor's voice provoke the silent dust,
    Or Flattery soothe the dull cold ear of Death?

Perhaps in this neglected spot is laid   45
    Some heart once pregnant with celestial fire;
Hands that the rod of empire might have swayed,
    Or waked to ecstasy the living lyre.

But Knowledge to their eyes her ample page
   Rich with the spoils of time did ne'er unroll;   50
Chill Penury repressed their noble rage,
   And froze the genial current of the soul.

Full many a gem of purest ray serene,
   The dark unfathomed caves of ocean bear:
Full many a flower is born to blush unseen,   55
   And waste its sweetness on the desert air.

Some village Hampden, that with dauntless breast
   The little tyrant of his fields withstood;
Some mute inglorious Milton here may rest,
   Some Cromwell guiltless of his country's blood.   60

The applause of listening senates to command,
   The threats of pain and ruin to despise,
To scatter plenty o'er a smiling land,
   And read their history in a nation's eyes,

Their lot forbade: nor circumscribed alone   65
   Their growing virtues, but their crimes confined;
Forbade to wade through slaughter to a throne,
   And shut the gates of mercy on mankind,

The struggling pangs of conscious truth to hide,
   To quench the blushes of ingenuous shame,   70
Or heap the shrine of Luxury and Pride
   With incense kindled at the Muse's flame.

Far from the madding crowd's ignoble strife,
   Their sober wishes never learned to stray;
Along the cool sequestered vale of life   75
   They kept the noiseless tenor of their way.

Yet even these bones from insult to protect
   Some frail memorial still erected nigh,
With uncouth rhymes and shapeless sculpture decked,
   Implores the passing tribute of a sigh.   80

Their name, their years, spelt by the unlettered Muse,
   The place of fame and elegy supply:
And many a holy text around she strews,
   That teach the rustic moralist to die.

For who to dumb Forgetfulness a prey,   85
   This pleasing anxious being e'er resigned,

Left the warm precincts of the cheerful day,
    Nor cast one longing lingering look behind?

On some fond breast the parting soul relies,
    Some pious drops the closing eye requires;   90
Even from the tomb the voice of Nature cries,
    Even in our ashes live their wonted fires.

For thee, who mindful of the unhonored dead
    Dost in these lines their artless tale relate;
If chance, by lonely contemplation led,   95
    Some kindred spirit shall inquire thy fate,

Haply some hoary-headed swain may say,
    "Oft have we seen him at the peep of dawn
Brushing with hasty steps the dews away
    To meet the sun upon the upland lawn.   100

"There at the foot of yonder nodding beech
    That wreathes its old fantastic roots so high,
His listless length at noontide would he stretch,
    And pore upon the brook that babbles by.

"Hard by yon wood, now smiling as in scorn,   105
    Muttering his wayward fancies he would rove,
Now drooping, woeful wan, like one forlorn,
    Or crazed with care, or crossed in hopeless love.

"One morn I missed him on the customed hill,
    Along the heath and near his favorite tree;
Another came; nor yet beside the rill,   110
    Nor up the lawn, nor at the wood was he;

"The next with dirges due in sad array
    Slow through the churchway path we saw him borne.
Approach and read (for thou canst read) the lay,   115
    Graved on the stone beneath yon aged thorn."

The Epitaph

Here rests his head upon the lap of Earth
    A youth to Fortune and to Fame unknown.
Fair Science frowned not on his humble birth,
    And Melancholy marked him for her own.   120

Large was his bounty, and his soul sincere,
    Heaven did a recompense as largely send:

He gave to Misery all he had, a tear,
He gained from Heaven ('twas all he wished) a friend.

No farther seek his merits to disclose, 125
Or draw his frailties from their dread abode
(There they alike in trembling hope repose),
The bosom of his Father and his God.

rude (l. 16): uneducated.   *horn* (l. 19): hunter's horn.   *glebe* (l. 26): soil.   *storied urn* (l. 41): funeral urn with an epitaph.   *animated* (l. 41): lifelike.   *Hampden* (l. 57): John Hampden, courageous opponent of Charles I. Killed in battle.   *Science* (l. 119): learning

Bells for John Whiteside's Daughter

John Crowe Ransom (1888–   )

There was such speed in her little body,
And such lightness in her footfall,
It is no wonder that her brown study
Astonishes us all.

Her wars were bruited in our high window. 5
We looked among orchard trees and beyond,
Where she took arms against her shadow,
Or harried unto the pond

The lazy geese, like a snow cloud
Dripping their snow on the green grass, 10
Tricking and stopping, sleepy and proud,
Who cried in goose, Alas,

For the tireless heart within the little
Lady with rod that made them rise
From their noon apple dreams, and scuttle 15
Goose-fashion under the skies!

But now go the bells, and we are ready;
In one house we are sternly stopped
To say we are vexed at her brown study,
Lying so primly propped. 20

The Lynching

Claude McKay (1890–1948)

His spirit in smoke ascended to high heaven.
His father, by the cruelest way of pain,
Had bidden him to his bosom once again;
The awful sin remained still unforgiven.
All night a bright and solitary star   5
(Perchance the one that ever guided him,
Yet gave him up at last to Fate's wild whim)
Hung pitifully o'er the swinging char.
Day dawned, and soon the mixed crowds came to view
The ghastly body swaying in the sun: 10
The women thronged to look, but never a one
Showed sorrow in her eyes of steely blue;
And little lads, lynchers that were to be,
Danced round the dreadful thing in fiendish glee.

Emmett Till

James A. Emanuel (1921–   )

I hear a whistling
Through the water.
Like Emmett
Won't be still.
He keeps floating   5
Round the darkness,
Edging through
The silent chill.

"The Lynching" from *Selected Poems of Claude McKay,* copyright 1953, reprinted by permission of Twayne Publishers, Inc.

"Emmett Till" from *The Treehouse and Other Poems,* Broadside Press, Detroit, 1968. Previously appeared in *The New York Times,* September 13, 1963. © 1963 by The New York Times Company. Reprinted by permission of The New York Times Company and James A. Emanuel.

83

Tell me, please,
That bedtime story   10
Of the fairy
River Boy
Who swims forever,
Deep in treasures,
Necklaced in   15
A coral toy.

title: In 1955, Emmett Till, a 14-year-old black youth, was kidnapped from his uncle's home in Sumner, Mississippi, for allegedly whistling at a white woman. His badly decomposed body was later recovered from the Tallahatchie River.

i saw them lynch

Carol Freeman (1941–   )

i saw them lynch festus whiteside and
all the limp white women with lymphatic greasy eyelids came
to watch silent silent in the dusty burning noon
shifting noiselessly from heavy foot to heavy
foot licking beast lips showing beast teeth in   5
anticipation of the feast
and they all plodded forward after the
lynching to grab and snatch the choice
pieces, rending them with their bloody teeth crunching on
    his hollow bones.   10

Between the World and Me

Richard Wright (1908–1960)

And one morning while in the woods I stumbled suddenly upon the thing,
Stumbled upon it in a grassy clearing guarded by scaly oaks and elms.
And the sooty details of the scene rose, thrusting themselves between the
    world and me. . . .

There was a design of white bones slumbering forgottenly upon a cushion of
    ashes.
There was a charred stump of a sapling pointing a blunt finger accusingly
    at the sky.   5
There were torn tree limbs, tiny veins of burnt leaves, and a scorched
    coil of greasy hemp;
A vacant shoe, an empty tie, a ripped shirt, a lonely hat, and a pair
    of trousers stiff with black blood.
And upon the trampled grass were buttons, dead matches, butt-ends of
    cigars and cigarettes, peanut shells, a drained gin-flask, and a whore's
    lipstick;
Scattered traces of tar, restless arrays of feathers, and the lingering smell
    of gasoline.
And through the morning air the sun poured yellow surprise into the eye
    sockets of a stony skull. . . .   10
And while I stood my mind was frozen with a cold pity for the life that
    was gone.
The ground gripped my feet and my heart was circled by icy walls of fear —
The sun died in the sky; a night wind muttered in the grass and fumbled
    the leaves in the trees; the woods poured forth the hungry yelping of
    hounds; the darkness screamed with thirsty voices; and the witnesses
    rose and lived:
The dry bones stirred, rattled, lifted, melting themselves into my bones.
The grey ashes formed flesh firm and black, entering into my flesh.   15
The gin-flask passed from mouth to mouth; cigars and cigarettes glowed,
    the whore smeared the lipstick red upon her lips,
And a thousand faces swirled around me, clamoring that my life be burned. . . .

And then they had me, stripped me, battering my teeth into my throat till
    I swallowed my own blood.
My voice was drowned in the roar of their voices, and my black wet body
    slipped and rolled in their hands as they bound me to the sapling.
And my skin clung to the bubbling hot tar, falling from me in limp patches. 20
And the down and quills of the white feathers sank into my raw flesh, and
    I moaned in my agony.
Then my blood was cooled mercifully, cooled by a baptism of gasoline.
And in a blaze of red I leaped to the sky as pain rose like water, boiling
    my limbs.
Panting, begging I clutched childlike, clutched to the hot sides of death.
Now I am dry bones and my face a stony skull staring in yellow surprise
    at the sun. . . .   25

When I Heard the Learn'd Astronomer

Walt Whitman (1819–1892)

When I heard the learn'd astronomer,
When the proofs, the figures, were ranged in columns before me,
When I was shown the charts and diagrams, to add, divide, and
    measure them,
When I sitting heard the astronomer where he lectured with much
    applause in the lecture-room,
How soon unaccountable I became tired and sick,   5
Till rising and gliding out I wander'd off by myself,
In the mystical moist night-air, and from time to time,
Look'd up in perfect silence at the stars.

Sonnet — To Science

Edgar Allan Poe (1809–1849)

Science! true daughter of Old Time thou art!
    Who alterest all things with thy peering eyes.
Why preyest thou thus upon the poet's heart,
    Vulture, whose wings are dull realities?
How should he love thee? or how deem thee wise,   5
    Who wouldst not leave him in his wandering
To seek for treasure in the jewelled skies,
    Albeit he soared with an undaunted wing?
Hast thou not dragged Diana from her car?
    And driven the Hamadryad from the wood   10
To seek a shelter in some happier star?
    Hast thou not torn the Naiad from her flood,
The Elfin from the green grass, and from me
The summer dream beneath the tamarind tree?

["Arcturus" is his other name—]

Emily Dickinson (1830–1886)

"Arcturus" is his other name—
I'd rather call him "Star."
It's very mean of Science
To go and interfere!

I slew a worm the other day—   5
A "Savan" passing by
Murmured "Resurgam"—"Centipede"!
"Oh Lord—how frail are we"!

I pull a flower from the woods—
A monster with a glass   10
Computes the stamens in a breath—
And has her in a "class"!

Whereas I took the Butterfly
Aforetime in my hat—
He sits erect in "Cabinets"—   15
The Clover bells forgot.

What once was "Heaven"
Is "Zenith" now—
Where I proposed to go
When Time's brief masquerade was done   20
Is mapped and charted too.

What if the poles sh'd frisk about
And stand upon their heads!
I hope I'm ready for "the worst"—
Whatever prank betides!   25

Perhaps the "Kingdom of Heaven's" changed—
I hope the "Children" there
Wont be "new fashioned" when I come—
And laugh at me—and stare—

I hope the Father in the skies   30
Will lift his little girl—
Old fashioned-naughty-everything—
Over the stile of "Pearl."

Credibility

John Ciardi (1916–   )

Who could believe an ant in theory?
a giraffe in blueprint?
Ten thousand doctors of what's possible
could reason half the jungle out of being.
I speak of love, and something more,   5
to say we are the thing that proves itself
not against reason, but impossibly true,
and therefore to teach reason reason.

A Projection

Reed Whittemore (1919–   )

I wish they would hurry up their trip to Mars,
Those rocket gentlemen.
We have been waiting too long; the fictions of little men
And canals,
And of planting and raising flags and opening markets   5
For beads, cheap watches, perfume and plastic jewelry —
All these begin to be tedious; what we need now
Is the real thing, a thoroughly bang-up voyage
Of discovery.

Led by Admiral Byrd   10
In the *Nina, Pinta* and *Santa Maria*
With a crew of one hundred experts
In physics, geology, war and creative writing,
The expedition should sail with a five-year supply of
Pemmican, Jello, Moxie,   15
Warm woolen socks and jars of Gramma's preserves.

Think of them out there,
An ocean of space before them, using no compass,
Guiding themselves by speculative equations,
Looking,   20
Looking into the night and thinking now
There are no days, no seasons, time
Is only on watches,
                    and landing on Venus
Through some slight error,
Bearing   25

Proclamations of friendship,
Declarations of interstellar faith,
Acknowledgments of American supremacy,
And advertising matter.

I wonder,   30
Out in the pitch of space, having worlds enough,
If the walled-up, balled-up self could from its alley
Sally.
I wish they would make provisions for this,
Those rocket gentlemen.   35

The Last Monster

John Montague (1930–   )

First, the dodo disappeared,
Leaving a legend of a simpleton's head,
Grotesque nut-cracker nose:
But a rum, a rare old one,
With feathers like old clothes.   5

The great Auk struck out for St. Kilda's,
Settled with shaggy highlanders,
Skin divers and such:
Learned the language of oblivion,
Finally lost touch.   10

Gone also, as Goldsmith noted,
The bird of Nazareth and the lesser tatou,
Beasts of strange pattern and birds past belief:
Even to number their names, like witchcraft,
Affords sensual relief.   15

Somewhere on the ultimate scarp,
The last monster watches
With hooded eyes,
While tiny men trek urgently towards him,
Armed with strange supplies.   20

Golden-pawed snowman of Everest,
Wildcat of the Grampians,
Lyre-bird of Peru:
Stay hidden wherever you are
The Abominable Scientist is after you!   25

Science

Robinson Jeffers (1887–1962)

Man, introverted man, having crossed
In passage and but a little with the nature of things this latter century
Has begot giants; but being taken up
Like a maniac with self-love and inward conflicts cannot manage his hybrids.
Being used to deal with edgeless dreams,   5
Now he's bred knives on nature turns them also inward: they have thirsty
    points though.
His mind forebodes his own destruction;
Actaeon who saw the goddess naked among leaves and his hounds tore him.
A little knowledge, a pebble from the shingle,
A drop from the oceans: who would have dreamed this infinitely little
    too much?   10

Dulce et Decorum Est

Wilfred Owen (1893–1918)

Bent double, like old beggars under sacks,
Knock-kneed, coughing like hags, we cursed through sludge,
Till on the haunting flares we turned our backs,
And towards our distant rest began to trudge.
Men marched asleep. Many had lost their boots,   5
But limped on, blood-shod. All went lame, all blind;
Drunk with fatigue; deaf even to the hoots
Of gas-shells dropping softly behind.

Gas! GAS! Quick, boys! — An ecstasy of fumbling,
Fitting the clumsy helmets just in time,   10
But someone still was yelling out and stumbling
And flound'ring like a man in fire or lime. —
Dim through the misty panes and thick green light,
As under a green sea, I saw him drowning.

In all my dreams before my helpless sight   15
He plunges at me, guttering, choking, drowning.

If in some smothering dreams, you too could pace
Behind the wagon that we flung him in,
And watch the white eyes writhing in his face,
His hanging face, like a devil's sick of sin,   20
If you could hear, at every jolt, the blood
Come gargling from the froth-corrupted lungs
Bitter as the cud
Of vile, incurable sores on innocent tongues, —
My friend, you would not tell with such high zest   25
To children ardent for some desperate glory,
The old lie: *Dulce et decorum est*
Pro patria mori.

title: "Dulce et decorum est pro patria mori," from the Latin poet Horace, means, "It is
sweet and fitting to die for one's country."

To Lucasta, Going to the Wars

Richard Lovelace (1618–1658)

Tell me not, sweet, I am unkind,
   That from the nunnery
Of thy chaste breast and quiet mind
   To war and arms I fly.

True, a new mistress now I chase,   5
   The first foe in the field;
And with a stronger faith embrace
   A sword, a horse, a shield.

Yet this inconstancy is such
   As thou too shalt adore: 10
I could not love thee, dear so much,
   Loved I not honor more.

The Death of the Ball Turret Gunner

Randall Jarrell (1914–1965)

From my mother's sleep I fell into the State,
And I hunched in its belly till my wet fur froze.
Six miles from earth, loosed from its dream of life,
I woke to black flak and the nightmare fighters.
When I died they washed me out of the turret with a hose.   5

The Fury of Aerial Bombardment

Richard Eberhart (1904–   )

You would think the fury of aerial bombardment
Would rouse God to relent; the infinite spaces
Are still silent. He looks on shock-pried faces.
History, even, does not know what is meant.

You would feel that after so many centuries   5
God would give man to repent; yet he can kill
As Cain could, but with multitudinous will,
No farther advanced than in his ancient furies.

Was man made stupid to see his own stupidity?
Is God by definition indifferent, beyond us all?   10
Is the eternal truth man's fighting soul
Wherein the Beast ravens in its own avidity?

Of Van Wettering I speak, and Averill,
Names on a list, whose faces I do not recall
But they are gone to early death, who late in school   15
Distinguished the belt feed lever from the belt holding pawl.

Old War-Dreams

Walt Whitman (1819–1892)

In midnight sleep of many a face of anguish,
Of the look at first of the mortally wounded, (of that indescribable look,)
Of the dead on their backs with arms extended wide,
        I dream, I dream, I dream.

Of scenes of Nature, fields and mountains,   5
Of skies so beauteous after a storm, and at night the moon so unearthly
        bright,
Shining sweetly, shining down, where we dig the trenches and gather
        the heaps,
        I dream, I dream, I dream.

Long have they pass'd, faces and trenches and fields,
Where through the carnage I moved with a callous composure,
    or away from the fallen,   10
Onward I sped at the time — but now of their forms at night,
    I dream, I dream, I dream.

One Morning We Brought Them Order

Al Lee (1938–   )

"With our considerable military power but limited political appeal, how do we contain
an adversary of enormous political power but modest military means?"

> *— An American military strategist quoted by*
> *Jean Lacouture in* Le Monde *(Sept. 18, 1964).*

When we rolled up the three armored vehicles
and they wouldn't budge, the sergeant said to kick
    in somebody's kidneys,
    and a corporal did.
It was a bald-headed man with a shiny   5
soft face. He sat tight but we could hear him whine.

  Our captain was somewhere else admiring
  and photographing a church's stone spire.
    It was famous or ancient.
    By the time he got back, rain   10
  was drenching them, and us, so he ordered
  us to hurry up and clobber some more.

    They still sat there, some not so pretty,
    when the colonel came. He had a fit.
      "Have it their way. Shoot a dozen   15
      in the head and see what that does."
    Then, pissed off that they kept on stalling,
    he had us open up on them all.

"One Morning We Brought Them Order" from *New American Review*, No. 3, reprinted by
permission of Al Lee.

Someone must have wanted to run
when we set to it. I wonder   20
why in all those thousands not one man
used his head and started the panic.
     He would have saved everyone's neck.
     Was what we did unexpected?

     We took chow thinking of them   25
     that night until the women
who had kept indoors at first came out too
to harass us by moonlight. The shooting
     lasted for hours. They fought back
     with knives and died attacking.   30

     After looting the town,
     we poured oil around it
and lit a fire to roast anybody's ass.
Today a young girl with a covered basket
     walked up smiling: she then   35
     exploded, killing ten.

The Great Day

W. B. Yeats (1865–1939)

Hurrah for revolution and more cannon-shot!
A beggar upon horseback lashes a beggar on foot.
Hurrah for revolution and cannon come again!
The beggars have changed places, but the lash goes on.

"The Great Day" reprinted with permission of The Macmillan Company, The Macmillan Company of Canada, and Mr. M. B. Yeats from *The Collected Poems of W. B. Yeats*. Copyright 1940 by Georgie Yeats, renewed 1968 by Bertha Georgie Yeats, Michael Butler Yeats, and Anne Yeats.

A Semi-Revolution

Robert Frost (1874–1963)

I advocate a semi-revolution.
The trouble with a total revolution
(Ask any reputable Rosicrucian)
Is that it brings the same class up on top.
Executives of skillful execution   5
Will therefore plan to go half-way and stop.
Yes, revolutions are the only salves,
But they're one thing that should be done by halves.

Rosicrucian (l. 3): Yeats belonged to the Rosicrucians, a group devoted to the practical application of occult philosophy to human affairs.

A Total Revolution

Oscar Williams (1900–   )

(An Answer for Robert Frost)

I advocate a total revolution.
The trouble with a semi-revolution,
It's likely to be slow as evolution.
Who wants to spend the ages in collusion
With Compromise, Complacence and Confusion?   5
As for the same class coming up on top
That's wholecloth from the propaganda shop;
The old saw says there's loads of room on top,
That's where the poor should really plan to stop.
And speaking of those people called the "haves,"   10
Who own the whole cow and must have the calves
(And plant the wounds so they can sell the salves)
They won't be stopped by doing things by halves.

I say that for a permanent solution
There's nothing like a total revolution!   15

P.S. And may I add by way of a conclusion
        I wouldn't dream to ask a Rosicrucian.

[Revolution is the Pod]

Emily Dickinson (1830–1886)

Revolution is the Pod
Systems rattle from
When the Winds of Will are stirred
Excellent is Bloom

But except its Russet Base   5
Every Summer be
The Entomber of itself,
So of Liberty —

Left inactive on the Stalk
All its Purple fled   10
Revolution shakes it for
Test if it be dead.

A Poison Tree

William Blake (1757–1827)

I was angry with my friend,
I told him my wrath, my wrath did end;
I was angry with my foe,
I told it not, my wrath did grow.

And I water'd it in fears,   5
Night and morning with my tears;
And I sunned it with smiles,
And with soft deceitful wiles.

And it grew both day and night,
Till it bore an apple bright;   10
And my foe beheld it shine,
And he knew that it was mine,

And into my garden stole
When the night had veil'd the pole:
In the morning glad I see   15
My foe outstretch'd beneath the tree

[Mine Enemy is growing old]

Emily Dickinson (1830–1886)

Mine Enemy is growing old —
I have at last Revenge —
The Palate of the Hate departs —
If any would avenge

Let him be quick — the Viand flits —   5
It is a faded Meat —
Anger as soon as fed is dead —
'Tis starving makes it fat —

The Compassionate Fool

Norman Cameron (1905–1953)

My enemy had bidden me as guest.
His table all set out with wine and cake,
His ordered chairs, he to beguile me dressed
So neatly, moved my pity for his sake.

"Mine Enemy is growing old" reprinted by permission of the publishers and the Trustees
of Amherst College from Thomas H. Johnson, Editor, The Poems of Emily Dickinson, Cam-
bridge, Mass.: The Belknap Press of Harvard University Press, copyright 1951, 1955 by
The President and Fellows of Harvard College.

"The Compassionate Fool" from Collected Poems by Norman Cameron reprinted by per-
mission of Mr. Alan Hodge and The Hogarth Press Ltd.

98

I knew it was an ambush, but could not   5
Leave him to eat his cake up by himself
And put his unused glasses on the shelf.
I made pretence of falling in his plot,

And trembled when in his anxiety
He bared it too absurdly to my view;   10
And even as he stabbed me through and through
I pitied him for his small strategy.

[What Soft-Cherubic Creatures—]

Emily Dickinson (1830–1886)

What Soft-Cherubic Creatures—
These Gentlewomen are—
One would as soon assault a Plush—
Or violate a Star—

Such Dimity Convictions—   5
A Horror so refined
Of freckled Human Nature—
Of Deity-ashamed—

It's such a common-Glory—
A Fisherman's-Degree—   10
Redemption-Brittle Lady—
Be so-ashamed of Thee—

the Cambridge ladies who live in furnished souls

e. e. cummings (1894–1962)

the Cambridge ladies who live in furnished souls
are unbeautiful and have comfortable minds
(also, with the church's protestant blessings
daughters, unscented shapeless spirited)
they believe in Christ and Longfellow, both dead,   5
are invariably interested in so many things—
at the present writing one still finds
delighted fingers knitting for the is it Poles?
perhaps. While permanent faces coyly bandy
scandal of Mrs. N and Professor D   10
. . . . the Cambridge ladies do not care, above
Cambridge if sometimes in its box of
sky lavender and cornerless, the
moon rattles like a fragment of angry candy

Miniver Cheevy

Edwin Arlington Robinson (1869–1935)

Miniver Cheevy, child of scorn,
   Grew lean while he assailed the seasons;
He wept that he was ever born,
   And he had reasons.

Miniver loved the days of old   5
   When swords were bright and steeds were prancing;
The vision of a warrior bold
   Would set him dancing.

Miniver sighed for what was not,
   And dreamed, and rested from his labors;   10
He dreamed of Thebes and Camelot,
   And Priam's neighbors.

Miniver mourned the ripe renown
    That made so many a name so fragrant;
He mourned Romance, now on the town,   15
    And Art, a vagrant.

Miniver loved the Medici,
    Albeit he had never seen one;
He would have sinned incessantly
    Could he have been one.   20

Miniver cursed the commonplace
    And eyed a khaki suit with loathing;
He missed the mediæval grace
    Of iron clothing.

Miniver scorned the gold he sought,   25
    But sore annoyed was he without it;
Miniver thought, and thought, and thought,
    And thought about it.

Miniver Cheevy, born too late,
    Scratched his head and kept on thinking;   30
Miniver coughed, and called it fate,
    And kept on drinking.

American Primitive

William Jay Smith (1918–   )

Look at him there in his stovepipe hat,
His high-top shoes, and his handsome collar;
Only my Daddy could look like that,
And I love my Daddy like he loves his Dollar.

The screen door bangs, and it sounds so funny—   5
There he is in a shower of gold;
His pockets are stuffed with folding money,
His lips are blue, and his hands feel cold.

He hangs in the hall by his black cravat,
The ladies faint, and the children holler: 10
Only my Daddy could look like that,
And I love my Daddy like he loves his Dollar.

The Scholars

W. B. Yeats (1865–1939)

Bald heads forgetful of their sins,
Old, learned, respectable bald heads
Edit and annotate the lines
That young men, tossing on their beds,
Rhymed out in love's despair   5
To flatter beauty's ignorant ear.

All shuffle there; all cough in ink;
All wear the carpet with their shoes;
All think what other people think;
All know the man their neighbor knows.   10
Lord, what would they say
Did their Catullus walk that way?

A Desperate Measure

Nigel Dennis (1912–   )

There are 86,400 seconds in every 24 hours;
Each second's tick marks the birth of 100 professors —
Id est, a daily 8,640,000 of 'em —
Emergent from wombs ranging from Chile to Birmingham.
An enormity, you cry? Excellent! You understand me.   5
Here are my well-argued reasons for believing that from now on
They should be strangled in their cradles, every last one:

102

In my distinguished decades as reviewer, critic, editor,
I have been obliged to read — and all of them by professors —
8,093 books or full-length studies about Kierkegaard;   10
9,002   "   "   "   "   "   Thackeray, Leopardi;
19,001 "   "   "   "   "   Dante, Goethe, Hardy.
About *Daniel Deronda* and the tireless George Eliot generally,
7,100 — which is understating her figure generously. Now, I
Will omit tons of other lumber of a like timber and go on   15
To cite briefly what I have had to stomach with acidity
Annually, in my long, honourable, dramaturgical capacity:

All the above added together and then some about Shakespeare;
Roughly the same with knobs on about Sophocles, Fletcher, Dekker,
Ibsen, Chekhov, Beckett, Sartre, Beaumont and Flecker,   20
O'Neill, Aeschylus, Pinter, Wesker — yea, yea, Wesker e'en.
These have fatigued me so disgustingly that there have been:

1,001 nights when I was impotent with women and had
Scarcely the zest to tackle even a small boy;
3,000 evenings when I threw up my hands,   25
4,000   "   "   " "   "   "   dinner.
Every one of those writings was done by a professor, except
When it was someone duller — I mean, Simone de Beauvoir:
Not a one of them showed any sign of caution or terror
At the prospect of the Last Judgment, *Dies Irae*, etcetera: 30
Not a one of them cared whether I plugged on or died,
Not " "   "   "   stopped short of 100,000 words:
Whence my cry to the world for professorial infanticide.

            Song

   They have nailed me to untenable hypotheses;
   They have used rusty six-inch nails from library doors;   35
   They have prodded my sides with interminable longueurs;
   They have soaked me with mugfuls of watered vinegar.
   Whole days that I might have spent in dancing and farting,
   They have obliged me to spend in fury, wincing and smarting.

Dr. Dawkins — a professor himself, but only at a dirty   40
University, a sort of seat where you buy your Ph.D. for money
And they put together your *Daniel Deronda* for you —
Dr. Dawkins has suggested that one per million dons should be spared
For reasons solely of historicity. Each faculty, the globe over,
Covering every tangible -osophy and -ology, should endeavour   45
To submit one professor for sparing, justifying this by arguing

His exemplary tedium, his cuneiform writing, his clay tablets. I
Respect Dawkins' integrity, but I shall not talk turkey:
Mercy is always impractical and never really necessary:
I know, as Herod did, that there is no time like infancy.   50

Permit me to ask, moreover, just how much mercy
Was ever proffered by a professor to the immortal dead?
Did he not grapple them from the quiet sea-bottom with dull hooks?
   "   "   "   dry their juices in the dark, to purvey as egg-powder?
   "   "   "   cook their sweetest simplicities into hashes of complexity?   55
I mention this fact so that you will be entirely reassured
That in demanding an overall death-sentence, I am not just selfish:
I am also mindful of others — of the phosphorescent lustre of corpuses.

"But will not many innocent babies who would never
Have grown up to be professors be strangled by mothers who are   60
Too impulsive by half, too spontaneous by nature?" Yes,
I grant this: now and then an infant that might have waxed
Into a bonny tax-collector, or a healthy Cuban guerrilla
Brutish enough to win the respect of Radicals the world over,
Will pay with his life for showing accidentally professorial stigma: —   65

Item: For dragging heavily on the delicious teat;
Item: For filling his diaper with impermeable solids;
Item: For looking, on being chucked, only glazed and stolid;
Item: For gnawing the same plastic ring with one-and-the-same grin;
Item: For eschewing the rich cluck, preferring the dense idiom.   70
But my breadth of vision allows me to shrug off injustices:
Such innocents will expire for the good of the whole — and not
So very many of them at that: normally you can trust any mother
To tell at a glance which child will be like which father or other.

"I shall not live to see this," I tell my son, "but it   = 75
Will come in your time." — "What!" he burbles:
"Not one more scramble through Blake's symbols?
  "   "   "   "   trample through Boswell's gambols?
  "   "   "   "   stumble over Howell and Lowell?
  "   "   "   "   rumble down Marx's *Capital*?   80
  "   "   "   "   fumble with Sainte-Beuve's genitals?
  "   "   "   "   Rimbaud round Verlaine's arsehole?"
"Nary a one," say I: "no worse pedantry shall be heard
Than the plod of the hippo and the fall of his turd."
"Blimey!" says he: "if what you say is really true, Dad,   85
Being crucified meanwhile won't feel any too bad."

104

Snapshot of a Pedant

George Garrett (1929–   )

Privately, your pencil makes
wry marginalia, doodles at the edge
of noted pages, underlines examples of
what you call the worst excesses.

"Puddles of Sentiment!" You scrawl   5
an epitaph for Shelley and his critics,
uneasy among the vague Romantics.

"Pope & Swift would have admired Bentley & Dennis
if only they had understood."
Thus gladly reconcile and make a peace   10
among the factions of your favorite century.

If I hide my mouth to laugh,
if I yawn, doze while you drone,
if, choking with frustration,
I curse you in the language of those years   15
for "a Blockhead and a fine dull Ass,"
I must (in truth) confess

your strictness is like a conscience,
your rigor's like the pattern which
the feet must follow in numbered silence   20
before they waltz free to real music.

One learns to count before one learns the dance.
One learns to speak grammatically before
one takes the stance of satire and/or praise.

And I have seen the virtue of   25
your passion for precision.
You teach, by vehement revision,
that labor is a way to love.

"Snapshot of a Pedant" from *New Poems by American Poets, No. 2*, ed. Ralph Humphries, Ballantine Books, 1957, reprinted by permission of George Garrett.

The Campus on the Hill

W. D. Snodgrass (1926–   )

Up the reputable walks of old established trees
They stalk, children of the *nouveaux riches;* chimes
Of the tall Clock Tower drench their heads in blessing:
"I don't wanna play at your house;
I don't like you any more."   5
My house stands opposite, on the other hill,
Among meadows, with the orchard fences down and falling;
Deer come almost to the door.
You cannot see it, even in this clearest morning.
White birds hang in the air between   10
Over the garbage landfill and those homes thereto adjacent,
Hovering slowly, turning, settling down
Like the flakes sifting imperceptibly onto the little town
In a waterball of glass.
And yet, this morning, beyond this quiet scene,   15
The floating birds, the backyards of the poor,
Beyond the shopping plaza, the dead canal, the hillside
      lying tilted in the air,
Tomorrow has broken out today:
Riot in Algeria, in Cyprus, in Alabama;
Aged in wrong, the empires are declining,   20
And China gathers, soundlessly, like evidence.
What shall I say to the young on such a morning? —
Mind is the one salvation? — also grammar? —
No; my little ones lean not toward revolt. They
Are the Whites, the vaguely furiously driven, who resist   25
Their souls with such passivity
As would make Quakers swear. All day, dear Lord, all day
They wear their godhead lightly.
They look out from their hill and say,
To themselves, "We have nowhere to go but down;   30
The great destination is to stay."
Surely the nations will be reasonable;
They look at the world — don't they? — the world's way?
The clock just now has nothing more to say.

April Inventory

W. D. Snodgrass (1926–   )

The green catalpa tree has turned
All white; the cherry blooms once more.
In one whole year I haven't learned
A blessed thing they pay you for.
The blossoms snow down in my hair;   5
The trees and I will soon be bare.

The trees have more than I to spare.
The sleek, expensive girls I teach,
Younger and pinker every year,
Bloom gradually out of reach.   10
The pear tree lets its petals drop
Like dandruff on a tabletop.

The girls have grown so young by now
I have to nudge myself to stare.
This year they smile and mind me how   15
My teeth are falling with my hair.
In thirty years I may not get
Younger, shrewder, or out of debt.

The tenth time, just a year ago,
I made myself a little list   20
Of all the things I'd ought to know;
Then told my parents, analyst,
And everyone who's trusted me
I'd be substantial, presently.

I haven't read one book about   25
A book or memorized one plot.
Or found a mind I didn't doubt.
I learned one date. And then forgot.
And one by one the solid scholars
Get the degrees, the jobs, the dollars.   30

And smile above their starchy collars.
I taught my classes Whitehead's notions;
One lovely girl, a song of Mahler's.

Lacking a source-book or promotions,
I showed one child the colors of
A luna moth and how to love. 35

I taught myself to name my name,
To bark back, loosen love and crying;
To ease my woman so she came,
To ease an old man who was dying. 40
I have not learned how often I
Can win, can love, but choose to die.

I have not learned there is a lie
Love shall be blonder, slimmer, younger;
That my equivocating eye 45
Loves only by my body's hunger;
That I have poems, true to feel,
Or that the lovely world is real.

While scholars speak authority
And wear their ulcers on their sleeves, 50
My eyes in spectacles shall see
These trees procure and spend their leaves.
There is a value underneath
The gold and silver in my teeth.

Though trees turn bare and girls turn wives, 55
We shall afford our costly seasons;
There is a gentleness survives
That will outspeak and has its reasons.
There is a loveliness exists,
Preserves us. Not for specialists. 60

['Truth is not the secret of a few']

Lawrence Ferlinghetti (1919–   )

      'Truth is not the secret of a few'
             yet
you would maybe think so
        the way some
    librarians   5
and cultural ambassadors and
      especially museum directors
            act

    you'd think they had a corner
          on it   10
    the way they
      walk around shaking
  their high heads and
      looking as if they never
  went to the bath   15
    room or anything

    But I wouldn't blame them
if I were you
    They say the Spiritual is best conceived
in abstract terms   20
    and then too
  walking around in museums always makes me
    want to
      'sit down'
  I always feel so   25
      constipated
  in those
    high altitudes

Museum Piece

Richard Wilbur (1921–   )

The good grey guardians of art
Patrol the halls on spongy shoes,
Impartially protective, though
Perhaps suspicious of Toulouse.

Here dozes one against the wall,   5
Disposed upon a funeral chair.
A Degas dancer pirouettes
Upon the parting of his hair.

See how she spins! The grace is there,
But strain as well is plain to see.   10
Degas loved the two together:
Beauty joined to energy.

Edgar Degas purchased once
A fine El Greco, which he kept
Against the wall beside his bed   15
To hang his pants on while he slept.

The Parable of the Old Man and the Young

Wilfred Owen (1893–1918)

So Abram rose, and clave the wood, and went,
And took the fire with him, and a knife.
And as they sojourned both of them together,
Isaac the first-born spake and said, "My Father,
Behold the preparations, fire and iron,   5
But where the lamb for this burnt-offering?"
Then Abram bound the youth with belts and straps,
And builded parapets and trenches there,
And stretched forth the knife to slay his son.

When lo! an angel called him out of heaven,   10
Saying, "Lay not thy hand upon the lad,
Neither do anything to him. Behold,
A ram, caught in a thicket by its horns;
Offer the Ram of Pride instead of him."
But the old man would not so, but slew his son, —   15
And half the seed of Europe, one by one.

See Genesis 22:1–18 for the story on which the poem is based.

Story of Isaac

Leonard Cohen (1934–   )

The door it opened slowly
   My father he came in
   I was nine years old
And he stood so tall above me
   Blue eyes they were shining   5
   And his voice was very cold.
Said, "I've had a vision
   And you know I'm strong and holy
   I must do what I've been told."
So he started up the mountain   10
   I was running he was walking   ﹨
   And his ax was made of gold.

The trees they got much smaller
   The lake a lady's mirror
   We stopped to drink some wine   15
Then he threw the bottle over
   Broke a minute later
   And he put his hand on mine.
Thought I saw an eagle
   But it might have been a vulture,   20
   I never could decide.
Then my father built an altar
   He looked once behind his shoulder
   He knew I would not hide.

You who build the altars now   25
   To sacrifice these children
   You must not do it any more.
A scheme is not a vision
   And you never have been tempted
   By a demon or a god.   30
You who stand above them now
   Your hatchets blunt and bloody,
   You were not there before.
When I lay upon a mountain
   And my father's hand was trembling   35
   With the beauty of the word.

And if you call me brother now
   Forgive me if I inquire
   Just according to whose plan?
When it all comes down to dust   40
   I will kill you if I must
   I will help you if I can.
When it all comes down to dust
   I will help you if I must
   I will kill you if I can.   45
And mercy on our uniform
Man of peace or man of war—
   The peacock spreads his fan.

See Genesis 22:1–18 for the story on which the poem is based.

[I like to see it lap the Miles]

Emily Dickinson (1830–1886)

I like to see it lap the Miles—
And lick the Valleys up—
And stop to feed itself at Tanks—
And then—prodigious step

Around a Pile of Mountains—   5
And supercilious peer
In Shanties—by the sides of Roads—
And then a Quarry pare

To fit its sides
And crawl between   10
Complaining all the while
In horrid-hooting stanza —
Then chase itself down Hill —

And neigh like Boanerges —
Then — prompter than a Star   15
Stop — docile and omnipotent
At its own stable door —

Boanerges (l. 13): presumably the name of a racehorse well-known in Emily Dickinson's
day.

To a Locomotive in Winter

Walt Whitman (1819–1892)

Thee for my recitative,
Thee in the driving storm even as now, the snow, the winter-day declining,
Thee in thy panoply, thy measur'd dual throbbing and thy beat convulsive,
Thy black cylindric body, golden brass and silvery steel,
Thy ponderous side-bars, parallel and connecting rods, gyrating, shuttling
    at thy sides,   5
Thy metrical, now swelling pant and roar, now tapering in the distance,
Thy great protruding head-light fix'd in front,
Thy long, pale, floating vapor-pennants, tinged with delicate purple,
The dense and murky clouds out-belching from thy smoke-stack,
Thy knitted frame, thy springs and valves, the tremulous twinkle of thy
    wheels,   10
Thy train of cars behind, obedient, merrily following,
Through gale or calm, now swift, now slack, yet steadily careering;
Type of the modern — emblem of motion and power — pulse of the continent,
For once come serve the Muse and merge in verse, even as here I see thee,
With storm and buffeting gusts of wind and falling snow,   15
By day thy warning ringing bell to sound its notes,
By night thy silent signal lamps to swing.
Fierce-throated beauty!
Roll through my chant with all thy lawless music, thy swinging lamps
    at night,
Thy madly-whistled laughter, echoing, rumbling like an earthquake,
    rousing all,   20
Law of thyself complete, thine own track firmly holding,
(No sweetness debonair of tearful harp or glib piano thine,)

Thy trills of shrieks by rocks and hills return'd,
Launch'd o'er the prairies wide, across the lakes,
To the free skies unpent and glad and strong.   25

The Express

Stephen Spender (1909–   )

After the first powerful plain manifesto
The black statement of pistons, without more fuss
But gliding like a queen, she leaves the station.
Without bowing and with restrained unconcern
She passes the houses which humbly crowd outside,   5
The gasworks and at last the heavy page
Of death, printed by gravestones in the cemetery.
Beyond the town there lies the open country
Where, gathering speed, she acquires mystery,
The luminous self-possession of ships on ocean.   10
It is now she begins to sing—at first quite low
Then loud, and at last with a jazzy madness—
The song of her whistle screaming at curves,
Of deafening tunnels, brakes, innumerable bolts.
And always light, aerial, underneath   15
Goes the elate meter of her wheels.
Steaming through metal landscape on her lines
She plunges new eras of wild happiness
Where speed throws up strange shapes, broad curves
And parallels clean like the steel of guns.   20
At last, further than Edinburgh or Rome,
Beyond the crest of the world, she reaches night
Where only a low streamline brightness
Of phosphorus on the tossing hills is white.
Ah, like a comet through flames she moves entranced   25
Wrapt in her music no bird song, no, nor bough
Breaking with honey buds, shall ever equal.

Departmental

Robert Frost (1874–1963)

An ant on the tablecloth
Ran into a dormant moth
Of many times his size.
He showed not the least surprise.
His business wasn't with such.   5
He gave it scarcely a touch,
And was off on his duty run.
Yet if he encountered one
Of the hive's enquiry squad
Whose work is to find out God   10
And the nature of time and space.
He would put him onto the case
Ants are a curious race;
One crossing with hurried tread
The body of one of their dead   15
Isn't given a moment's arrest—
Seems not even impressed.
But he no doubt reports to any
With whom he crosses antennae,
And they no doubt report   20
To the higher up at court.
Then word goes forth in Formic:
"Death's come to Jerry McCormic,
Our selfless forager Jerry.
Will the special Janizary   25
Whose office it is to bury
The dead of the commissary
Go bring him home to his people.
Lay him in state on a sepal.
Wrap him for shroud in a petal.   30
Embalm him with ichor of nettle.
This is the word of your Queen."
And presently on the scene
Appears a solemn mortician;
And taking formal position   35
With feelers calmly atwiddle,
Seizes the dead by the middle,

And heaving him high in air,
Carries him out of there.
No one stands round to stare.   40
It is nobody else's affair.

It couldn't be called ungentle.
But how thoroughly departmental.

The Unknown Citizen

W. H. Auden (1907–   )

(To JS/07/M/378
This Marble Monument
Is Erected by the State)

He was found by the Bureau of Statistics to be
One against whom there was no official complaint,
And all the reports on his conduct agree
That, in the modern sense of an old-fashioned word, he was a saint,
For in everything he did he served the Greater Community.   5
Except for the War till the day he retired
He worked in a factory and never got fired,
But satisfied his employers, Fudge Motors Inc.
Yet he wasn't a scab or odd in his views,
For his Union reports that he paid his dues,   10
(Our report on his Union shows it was sound)
And our Social Psychology workers found
That he was popular with his mates and liked a drink.
The Press are convinced that he bought a paper every day
And that his reactions to advertisements were normal in every way.   15
Policies taken out in his name prove that he was fully insured,
And his Health-card shows he was once in hospital but left it cured.
Both Producers Research and High-Grade Living declare
He was fully sensible to the advantages of the Installment Plan
And had everything necessary to the Modern Man,   20
A phonograph, a radio, a car and a frigidaire.
Our researchers into Public Opinion are content
That he held the proper opinions for the time of year;
When there was peace, he was for peace; when there was war, he went.

116

He was married and added five children to the population,   25
Which our Eugenist says was the right number for a parent of his generation,
And our teachers report that he never interfered with their education.
Was he free? Was he happy? The question is absurd:
Had anything been wrong, we should certainly have heard.

Leisure

W. H. Davies (1870–1940)

What is this life, if, full of care,
We have no time to stand and stare,

No time to stand beneath the boughs
And stare as long as sheep or cows.

No time to see, when woods we pass,   5
Where squirrels hide their nuts in grass.

No time to see, in broad daylight,
Streams full of stars, like skies at night.

No time to turn at Beauty's glance,
And watch her feet, how they can dance.   10

No time to wait till her mouth can
Enrich that smile her eyes began.

A poor life this if, full of care,
We have no time to stand and stare.

The Way We Wonder

Robert Pack (1929–   )

What has become of our astonishment
For simple things: colors, sounds, the hour of day?
We wonder, now our early gift is spent,

About imagined reasons to repent
For joy, and words we've heard our parents say.   5
What has become of our astonishment

For night and stars and things we can't invent?
(While crickets tick the perfect night away.)
We wonder, now our early gift is spent,

Whether some miraculous event   10
Will soon reveal (we're told old men are gay)
What has become of our astonishment.

The questioning of ultimate intent
Is still continued in the abstract way
We wonder, now our early gift is spent.   15

O who among us would have ever dreamt
The very best of our ideas betray?
What has become of our astonishment
We wonder, now our early gift is spent.

The World is Too Much with Us

William Wordsworth (1770–1850)

The world is too much with us: late and soon,
Getting and spending, we lay waste our powers:
Little we see in Nature that is ours;
We have given our hearts away, a sordid boon!
This Sea that bares her bosom to the moon;   5
The winds that will be howling at all hours,
And are up-gathered now like sleeping flowers;

"The Way We Wonder" reprinted by permission of Charles Scribner's Sons from *The Irony of Joy: Poems* by Robert Pack. Copyright 1955 by Robert Pack. (*Poets of Today II.*)

For this, for everything, we are out of tune;
It moves us not.—Great God! I'd rather be
A Pagan suckled in a creed outworn;   10
So might I, standing on this pleasant lea,
Have glimpses that would make me less forlorn;
Have sight of Proteus rising from the sea;
Or hear old Triton blow his wreathed horn.

Pied Beauty

Gerard Manley Hopkins (1844–1889)

Glory be to God for dappled things—
    For skies of couple-colour as a brindled cow;
        For rose-moles all in stipple upon trout that swim
Fresh-firecoal chestnut-falls; finches wings;
    Landscape plotted and pieced—fold, fallow, and plough;   5
        And all trades, their gear and tackle and trim.

All things, counter, original, spare, strange;
    Whatever is fickle, freckled (who knows how?)
        With swift, slow; sweet, sour; adazzle, dim;
He fathers-forth whose beauty is past change: 10
                    Praise him.

Ode on a Grecian Urn

John Keats (1795–1821)

Thou still unravished bride of quietness,
    Thou foster-child of silence and slow time,
Sylvan historian, who canst thus express
    A flowery tale more sweetly than our rhyme:
What leaf-fringed legend haunts about thy shape   5
    Of deities or mortals, or of both,
        In Tempe or the dales of Arcady?
    What men or gods are these? What maidens loth?
What mad pursuit? What struggle to escape?
        What pipes and timbrels? What wild ecstasy?   10

Heard melodies are sweet, but those unheard
   Are sweeter; therefore, ye soft pipes, play on;
Not to the sensual ear, but, more endeared,
   Pipe to the spirit ditties of no tone:
Fair youth, beneath the trees, thou canst not leave   15
   Thy song, nor ever can those trees be bare;
     Bold Lover, never, never canst thou kiss,
Though winning near the goal — yet, do not grieve;
    She cannot fade, though thou hast not thy bliss,
   For ever wilt thou love, and she be fair!   20

Ah, happy, happy boughs! that cannot shed
   Your leaves, nor ever bid the Spring adieu;
And, happy melodist, unwearièd,
   For ever piping songs for ever new;
More happy love! more happy, happy love!   25
   For ever warm and still to be enjoyed,
    For ever panting, and for ever young;
All breathing human passion far above,
   That leaves a heart high-sorrowful and cloyed,
    A burning forehead, and a parching tongue.   30

Who are these coming to the sacrifice?
   To what green altar, O mysterious priest,
Lead'st thou that heifer lowing at the skies,
   And all her silken flanks with garlands drest?
What little town by river or sea shore,   35
   Or mountain-built with peaceful citadel,
    Is emptied of this folk, this pious morn?
And, little town, thy streets for evermore
   Will silent be; and not a soul to tell
    Why thou art desolate, can e'er return.   40

O Attic shape! Fair attitude! with brede
   Of marble men and maidens overwrought,
With forest branches and the trodden weed;
   Thou, silent form, dost tease us out of thought
As doth Eternity: Cold Pastoral!   45
   When old age shall this generation waste,
    Thou shalt remain, in midst of other woe
   Than ours, a friend to man, to whom thou say'st,
Beauty is truth, truth beauty, — that is all
    Ye know on earth, and all ye need to know.   50

Lapis Lazuli

W. B. Yeats (1865–1939)

(For Harry Clifton)

I have heard that hysterical women say
They are sick of the palette and fiddle-bow,
Of poets that are always gay,
For everybody knows or else should know
That if nothing drastic is done   5
Aeroplane and Zeppelin will come out,
Pitch like King Billy bomb-balls in
Until the town lie beaten flat.

All perform their tragic play,
There struts Hamlet, there is Lear,   10
That's Ophelia, that Cordelia;
Yet they, should the last scene be there,
The great stage curtain about to drop,
If worthy their prominent part in the play,
Do not break up their lines to weep.   15
They know that Hamlet and Lear are gay;
Gaiety transfiguring all that dread.
All men have aimed at, found and lost;
Black out; Heaven blazing into the head:
Tragedy wrought to its uttermost.   20
Though Hamlet rambles and Lear rages,
And all the drop-scenes drop at once
Upon a hundred thousand stages,
It cannot grow by an inch or an ounce.

On their own feet they came, or on shipboard,   25
Camel-back, horse-back, ass-back, mule-back,
Old civilisations put to the sword.
Then they and their wisdom went to rack:
No handiwork of Callimachus,
Who handled marble as if it were bronze,   30
Made draperies that seemed to rise
When sea-wind swept the corner, stands;
His long lamp-chimney shaped like the stem
Of a slender palm, stood but a day;
All things fall and are built again,   35
And those that build them again are gay.

Two Chinamen, behind them a third,
Are carved in lapis lazuli,
Over them flies a long-legged bird,
A symbol of longevity;   40
The third, doubtless a serving-man,
Carries a musical instrument.

Every discoloration of the stone,
Every accidental crack or dent,
Seems a water-course or an avalanche,   45
Or lofty slope where it still snows
Though doubtless plum or cherry-branch
Sweetens the little half-way house
Those Chinamen climb towards, and I
Delight to imagine them seated there;   50
There, on the mountain and the sky,
On all the tragic scene they stare.
One asks for mournful melodies;
Accomplished fingers begin to play.
Their eyes mid many wrinkles, their eyes,   55
Their ancient, glittering eyes, are gay.

Easter Wings

George Herbert (1593–1633)

Lord, who createdst man in wealth and store,
  Though foolishly he lost the same,
    Decaying more and more
      Till he became
        Most poor: 5
        With Thee
       O let me rise
     As larks, harmoniously,
  And sing this day Thy victories:
Then shall the fall further the flight in me.   10

My tender age in sorrow did begin:
  And still with sickness and shame
    Thou didst so punish sin
      That I became
        Most thin.   15
        With Thee
       Let me combine,
     And feel this day Thy victory;
  For, if I imp my wing on Thine,
Affliction shall advance the flight in me.   20

The Contrite Heart

William Cowper (1731–1800)

The Lord will happiness divine
   On contrite hearts bestow:
Then tell me, gracious God, is mine
   A contrite heart, or no?

I hear, but seem to hear in vain,   5
   Insensible as steel;
If ought is felt, 'tis only pain,
   To feel I cannot feel.

I sometimes think myself inclin'd
   To love thee, if I could;   10
But often feel another mind,
   Averse to all that's good.

My best desires are faint and few,
   I fain would strive for more;
But when I cry, 'My strength renew,'   15
   Seem weaker than before.

Thy saints are comforted I know,
   And love thy house of pray'r;
I therefore go where others go,
   But find no comfort there.   20

Oh make this heart rejoice, or ache;
   Decide this doubt for me;
And if it be not broken, break,
   And heal it, if it be.

[Thou art indeed just, Lord]

Gerard Manley Hopkins (1844–1889)

Justus quidem tu es, Domine, si disputem tecum: verumtamen justa loquar ad te: Quare via impiorum prosperatur? &c.

Thou are indeed just, Lord, if I contend
With thee; but, sir, so what I plead is just.
Why do sinners' ways prosper? and why must
Disappointment all I endeavor end?
   Wert thou my enemy, O thou my friend,   5

How wouldst thou worse, I wonder, than thou dost
Defeat, thwart me? Oh, the sots and thralls of lust
Do in spare hours more thrive than I that spend,
Sir, life upon thy cause. See, banks and brakes
Now, leavèd how thick! lacèd they are again   10
With fretty chervil, look, and fresh wind shakes
Them; birds build—but not I build; no, but strain,
Time's eunuch, and not breed one work that wakes.
Mine, O thou lord of life, send my roots rain.

The first three lines of the sonnet translate the Latin epigraph.

[My lady's presence makes the roses red]

Henry Constable (1567?–1627)

My lady's presence makes the roses red,
Because to see her lips they blush for shame.
The lily's leaves, for envy, pale became,
And her white hands in them this envy bred.
The marigold the leaves abroad doth spread,   5
Because the sun's and her power is the same.
The violet of purple colour came,
Dyed in the blood she made my heart to shed.
In brief: all flowers from her their virtue take;
From her sweet breath their sweet smells do proceed;   10
The living heat which her eyebeams doth make
Warmeth the ground, and quickeneth the seed.
    The rain, wherewith she watereth the flowers,
    Falls from mine eyes, which she dissolves in showers.

[My mistress' eyes are nothing like the sun]

William Shakespeare (1564–1616)

My mistress' eyes are nothing like the sun;
Coral is far more red than her lips red;
If snow be white, why then her breasts are dun;
If hairs be wires, black wires grow on her head.

I have seen roses damasked, red and white,   5
But no such roses see I in her cheeks;
And in some perfumes is there more delight
Than in the breath that from my mistress reeks.
I love to hear her speak, yet well I know
That music hath a far more pleasing sound;   10
I grant I never saw a goddess go;
My mistress, when she walks, treads on the ground.
And yet, by heaven, I think my love as rare
As any she belied with false compare.

It Is a Beauteous Evening

William Wordsworth (1770–1850)

It is a beauteous evening, calm and free,
The holy time is quiet as a Nun
Breathless with adoration; the broad sun
Is sinking down in its tranquillity;
The gentleness of heaven broods o'er the Sea;   5
Listen! the mighty Being is awake,
And doth with his eternal motion make
A sound like thunder—everlastingly.
Dear Child! Dear Girl! that walkest with me here,
If thou appear untouched by solemn thought,   10
Thy nature is not therefore less divine:
Thou liest in Abraham's bosom all the year;
And Worship'st at the Temple's inner shrine,
God being with thee when we know it not.

Abraham's bosom (l. 12): see Luke 16:22.

125

Country Club Sunday

Phyllis McGinley (1905–   )

It is a beauteous morning, calm and free.
    The fairways sparkle. Gleam the shaven grasses.
Mirth fills the locker rooms and, hastily,
    Stewards fetch ice, fresh towels, and extra glasses.

On terraces the sandaled women freshen   5
    Their lipstick; gather to gossip, poised and cool;
And the shrill adolescent takes possession,
    Plunging and splashing, of the swimming pool.

It is a beauteous morn, opinion grants.
    Nothing remains of last night's Summer Formal   10
Save palms and streamers and the wifely glance,
    Directed with more watchfulness than normal,
At listless mate who tugs his necktie loose,
Moans, shuns the light, and gulps tomato juice.

Five

Poetry and the Fine Arts

Though there has been much study of the subject, poetic creation remains something of a mystery. Some poems very likely get written in a blaze of inspiration, but the evidence is overwhelming that most poems are the result of painstaking and protracted revision. More often than not, the poet travels a long road to the finished poem.

Where does that road begin? That too is often a mystery—even to the poet himself. We can turn to the poets' notebooks, journals, and letters (if they are available) and perhaps find what we are looking for. We can read the accounts a few poets have published about particular poems. And we can examine the life of a poet on the reasonable assumption that it will yield clues and suggestions about the inspiration of particular works. But such a quest is obviously taking us farther and farther away from the poem. Though we will readily agree that what we might discover in letters, journals, essays, and biographies will have some relevance to the poem we began with, we might stop at some point, look back at the poem receding in the distance, and wonder if it is worthwhile trying to discover where the road begins. We want to enjoy poetry, not become scholar-biographers and amateur psychologists.

The poems in this chapter offer one kind of solution to the problem. All were inspired by a specific painting or sculpture that the poem deals with in detail. We can therefore keep before us and study the inspiration while we are studying the poem. The poet has gazed upon a painting and been moved deeply enough to give shape and form to the feelings inspired by the encounter. He has broken the silence of the painting, given it words.

127

Of course, it is the words the poet has given the painting that are important — that is, the poem as a poem. To say that William Carlos Williams was inspired to write "The Dance" by Brueghel's painting "The Kermess" is obviously correct and obviously not very significant. By inspiration, we clearly mean something more significant: Was Williams inspired by Brueghel's harmonies of color or sense of movement? Did the painting perhaps inspire the poet to a technical challenge, to see whether he could convey in words the sense of the painting's motion and circularity? When we discuss inspiration in this sense, we are also discussing the poem as a poem.

The poem, then, can be seen as a kind of dialogue with the painting, a dialogue that you can enter into. And since all of the paintings are great works in their own right, the dialogue need not be dominated by the voice of the poet — although our interest is primarily in poetry. You will find yourself asking many questions about the poems: Are they successful (or even comprehensible) without reference to the paintings? Is the poet attempting an accurate and neutral verbal description of the painting or is he also making some judgment about it? Why does the poet choose to emphasize certain details of a painting and ignore others? What accounts for the order in which the poet deals with the details of the painting? (Useful here would be a comparison of the poems inspired by the same painting.) Do you feel that the poet at times is reading more into the painting than is warranted or that he is misreading the painting? Finally and more generally, do you feel that the poems are weak because they were inspired by works of art rather than by life?

The Bronze David of Donatello

Randall Jarrell (1914–1965)

A sword in his right hand, a stone in his left hand,
He is naked. Shod and naked. Hatted and naked.
The ribbons of his leaf-wreathed, bronze-brimmed bonnet
Are tasseled; crisped into the folds of frills,
Trills, graces, they lie in separation   5
Among the curls that lie in separation
Upon the shoulders.
                    Lightly, as if accustomed,
Loosely, as if indifferent,
The boy holds in grace
The stone moulded, somehow, by the fingers,   10
The sword alien, somehow, to the hand.
                            The boy David
Said of it: "There is none like *that*."
                           The boy David's
Body shines in freshness, still unhandled,
And thrusts its belly out a little in exact
Shamelessness. Small, close, complacent,   15
A labyrinth the gaze retraces,
The rib-case, navel, nipples are the features
Of a face that holds us like the whore Medusa's—
Of a face that, like the genitals, is sexless.
What sex has victory?   20
The mouth's cut Cupid's-bow, the chin's unwinning dimple
Are tightened, a little oily, take, use, notice:
Centering itself upon itself, the sleek
Body with its too-large head, this green
Fruit now forever green, this offending   25
And efficient elegance draws subtly, supply,
Between the world and itself, a shining
Line of delimitation, demarcation.
The body mirrors itself.
                    Where the armpit becomes breast,
Becomes back, a great crow's-foot is slashed.   30
Yet who would gash
The sleek flesh so? the cast, filed, shining flesh?
The cuts are folds: these are the folds of flesh
That closes on itself as a knife closes.

David by Donatello. Bronze. Mus. Nazionale, Florence. Courtesy Alinari–Art Reference Bureau.

To so much strength, those overborne by it   35
Seemed girls, and death came to it like a girl,
Came to it, through the soft air, like a bird —
So that the boy is like a girl, is like a bird
Standing on something it has pecked to death.

The boy stands at ease, his hand upon his hip: 40
The truth of victory. A Victory
Angelic, almost, in indifference,
An angel sent with no message but this triumph
And alone, now, in his triumph,
He looks down at the head and does not see it.   45

Upon this head
As upon a spire, the boy David dances,
Dances, and is exalted.
                        Blessed are those brought low,
Blessed is defeat, sleep blessed, blessed death.

The right foot is planted on a wing. Bent back in ease   50
Upon a supple knee — the toes curl a little, grasping
The crag upon which they are set in triumph —
The left leg glides toward, the left foot lies upon
A head. The head's other wing (the head is bearded
And winged and helmeted and bodiless)   55
Grows like a swan's wing up inside the leg;
Clothes, as the suit of a swan-maiden clothes,
The leg. The wing reaches, almost, to the rounded
Small childish buttocks. The dead wing warms the leg,
The dead wing, crushed beneath the foot, is swan's-down.   60
Pillowed upon the rock, Goliath's head
Lies under the foot of David.

Strong in defeat, in death rewarded,
The head dreams what has destroyed it
And is untouched by its destruction.   65
The stone sunk in the forehead, say the Scriptures;
There is no stone in the forehead. The head is helmed
Or else, unguarded, perfect still.
Borne high, borne long, borne in mastery,
The head is fallen.
                    The new light falls   70
As if in tenderness, upon the face —
Its masses shift for a moment, like an animal,
And settle, misshapen, into sleep: Goliath
Snores a little in satisfaction.

The story of David and Goliath is told in I Samuel 17.

131

Venus and the Lute Player by Titian (Tiziano Vecelli). Oil on canvas. 65″ × 82½″. The Metropolitan Museum of Art, Munsey Fund, 1936.

Venus and the Lute Player

Paul Engle (1908–   )

(Tiziano Vecellio, 1477–1576)

Far in the background a blue mountain waits
To echo back the song.
The note-necked swan, while it reverberates,
Paddles the tune along.

The player is a young man richly dressed.   5
His hand is never mute.
But quick in motion as if it caressed
Both lady and the lute.

Nude as the sunlit air the lady rests.
She does not listen with her dainty ear,   10
But trembles at the love song as her breasts
Turn pink to hear.

She does not rise up at his voice's fall,
But takes that music in,
By pointed leg and searching hand, with all   15
Her naked skin.

Out of that scene, far off, her hot eyes fall,
Hoping they will take in
The nearing lover, whom she can give all
Her naked skin.   20

133

Fall of Icarus by Brueghel. Beaux Arts, Brussels. Courtesy Marburg–Art Reference Bureau.

Musée des Beaux Arts

W. H. Auden (1907–   )

About suffering they were never wrong,
The old Masters: how well they understood
Its human position: how it takes place
While someone else is eating or opening a window or just walking dully along;
How, when the aged are reverently, passionately waiting   5
For the miraculous birth, there always must be
Children who did not specially want it to happen, skating
On a pond at the edge of the wood:
They never forgot
That even the dreadful martyrdom must run its course   10
Anyhow in a corner, some untidy spot
Where the dogs go on with their doggy life and the torturer's horse
Scratches its innocent behind on a tree.
In Breughel's *Icarus*, for instance: how everything turns away
Quite leisurely from the disaster; the ploughman may   15
Have heard the splash, the forsaken cry,
But for him it was not an important failure; the sun shone
As it had to on the white legs disappearing into the green
Water, and the expensive delicate ship that must have seen
Something amazing, a boy falling out of the sky,   20
Had somewhere to get to and sailed calmly on.

Landscape with the Fall of Icarus

William Carlos Williams (1883–1963)

According to Brueghel
when Icarus fell
it was spring

a farmer was ploughing
his field   5
the whole pageantry

Kermesse by Brueghel. Kunsthistorisches, Vienna. Courtesy Marburg–Art Reference Bureau.

of the year was
awake tingling
with itself

sweating in the sun   10
that melted
the wings' wax

unsignificantly
off the coast
there was   15

a splash quite unnoticed
this was
Icarus drowning

The Dance

William Carlos Williams (1883–1963)

In Breughel's great picture, The Kermess,
the dancers go round, they go round and
around, the squeal and the blare and the
tweedle of bagpipes, a bugle and fiddles
tipping their bellies (round as the thick-   5
sided glasses whose wash they impound)
their hips and their bellies off balance
to turn them. Kicking and rolling about
the Fair Grounds, swinging their butts, those
shanks must be sound to bear up under such   10
rollicking measures, prance as they dance
in Breughel's great picture, The Kermess.

Hunters in the Snow: Brueghel

Joseph Langland (1917–   )

Quail and rabbit hunters with tawny hounds,
Shadowless, out of late afternoon
Trudge toward the neutral evening of indeterminate form.
Done with their blood-annunciated day
Public dogs and all the passionless mongrels   5
Through deep snow
Trail their deliberate masters
Descending from the upper village home in lovering light.
Sooty lamps
Glow in the stone-carved kitchens.   10

This is the fabulous hour of shape and form
When Flemish children are gray-black-olive
And green-dark-brown
Scattered and skating informal figures
On the mill ice pond.   15
Moving in stillness
A hunched dame struggles with her bundled sticks,
Letting her evening's comfort cudgel her
While she, like jug or wheel, like a wagon cart
Walked by lazy oxen along the old snowlanes,   20
Creeps and crunches down the dusky street.
High in the fire-red dooryard
Half unhitched the sign of the Inn
Hangs in wind
Tipped to the pitch of the roof.   25
Near it anonymous parents and peasant girl,
Living like proverbs carved in the alehouse walls,
Gather the country evening into their arms
And lean to the glowing flames.

Now in the dimming distance fades   30
The other village; across the valley
Imperturbable Flemish cliffs and crags
Vaguely advance, close in, loom
Lost in nearness. Now
The night-black raven perched in branching boughs   35
Opens its early wing and slipping out
Above the gray-green valley
Weaves a net of slumber over the snow-capped homes.

138

Hunters in the Snow by Brueghel. Kunsthistorisches, Vienna. Courtesy Wolfrum–Art Reference Bureau.

And now the church, and then the walls and roofs
Of all the little houses are become   40
Close kin to shadow with small lantern eyes.
And now the bird of evening
With shadows streaming down from its gliding wings
Circles the neighboring hills
Of Hertogenbosch, Brabant.   45

Darkness stalks the hunters,
Slowly sliding down,
Falling in beating rings and soft diagonals.
Lodged in the vague vast valley the village sleeps.

Winter Landscape

John Berryman (1914–1972)

The three men coming down the winter hill
In brown, with tall poles and a pack of hounds
At heel, through the arrangement of the trees,
Past the five figures at the burning straw,
Returning cold and silent to their town,   5

Returning to the drifted snow, the rink
Lively with children, to the older men,
The long companions they can never reach,
The blue light, men with ladders, by the church
The sledge and shadow in the twilit street,   10

Are not aware that in the sandy time
To come, the evil waste of history
Outstretched, they will be seen upon the brow
Of that same hill: when all their company
Will have been irrecoverably lost,   15

These men, this particular three in brown
Witnessed by birds will keep the scene and say
By their configuration with the trees,
The small bridge, the red houses and the fire,
What place, what time, what morning occasion   20

Sent them into the wood, a pack of hounds
At heel and the tall poles upon their shoulders,
Thence to return as now we see them and
Ankle-deep in snow down the winter hill
Descend, while three birds watch and the fourth flies.   25

Brueghel's Winter

Walter de la Mare (1867–1900)

Jagg'd mountain peaks and skies ice-green
Wall in the wild, cold scene below.
Churches, farms, bare copse, the sea
In freezing quiet of winter show;
Where ink-black shapes on fields in flood   5
Curling, skating, and sliding go.
To left, a gabled tavern; a blaze;
Peasants; a watching child; and lo,
Muffled, mute—beneath naked trees
In sharp perspective set a-row—   10
Trudge huntsmen, sinister spears aslant,
Dogs snuffling behind them in the snow;
And arrowlike, lean, athwart the air
    Swoops into space a crow.

But flame, nor ice, nor piercing rock,   15
Nor silence, as of a frozen sea,
Nor that slant inward infinite line
Of signboard, bird, and hill, and tree,
Give more than subtle hint of him
Who squandered here life's mystery.   20

The Great Wave at Kamagawa by Katsushika Hokusai. Dated 1823–29. Woodprint. The Metropolitan Museum of Art, The Howard Mansfield Collection, Rogers Fund, 1936.

The Great Wave: Hokusai

Donald Finkel (1929–   )

But we will take the problem in its most obscure manifestation, and suppose that our spectator is an average Englishman. A trained observer, carefully hidden behind a screen, might notice a dilation in his eyes, even an intake of his breath, perhaps a grunt.

— Herbert Read, *The Meaning of Art*

It is because the sea is blue,
Because Fuji is blue, because the bent blue
Men have white faces, like the snow
On Fuji, like the crest of the wave in the sky the color of their
Boats. It is because the air   5
Is full of writing, because the wave is still: that nothing
Will harm these frail strangers,
That high over Fuji in an earthcolored sky the fingers
Will not fall; and the blue men
Lean on the sea like snow, and the wave like a mountain leans   10
Against the sky.

           In the painter's sea
All fishermen are safe. All anger bends under his unity.
But the innocent bystander, he merely
'Walks round a corner, thinking of nothing': hidden   15
Behind a screen we hear his cry.
He stands half in and half out of the world; he is the men,
But he cannot see below Fuji
The shore the color of sky; he is the wave, he stretches
His claws against strangers. He is   20
Not safe, not even from himself. His world is flat.
He fishes a sea full of serpents, he rides his boat
Blindly from wave to wave toward Ararat.

Man with Hoe by Millet. Private Collection. Courtesy Marburg–Art Reference Bureau.

The Man with the Hoe

Edwin Markham (1852–1940)

God made man in His own image
In the image of God He made him.
— *Genesis*

Bowed by the weight of centuries he leans
Upon his hoe and gazes on the ground,
The emptiness of ages in his face,
And on his back the burden of the world.
Who made him dead to rapture and despair,   5
A thing that grieves not and that never hopes,
Stolid and stunned, a brother to the ox?
Who loosened and let down this brutal jaw?
Whose was the hand that slanted back this brow?
Whose breath blew out the light within this brain?   10

Is this the Thing the Lord God made and gave
To have dominion over sea and land;
To trace the stars and search the heavens for power;
To feel the passion of Eternity?
Is this the dream He dreamed who shaped the suns   15
And markt their ways upon the ancient deep?
Down all the caverns of Hell to their last gulf
There is no shape more terrible than this—
More tongued with censure of the world's blind greed—
More filled with signs and portents for the soul—   20
More packt with danger to the universe.

What gulfs between him and the seraphim!
Slave of the wheel of labor, what to him
Are Plato and the swing of Pleiades?
What the long reaches of the peaks of song,   25
The rife of dawn, the reddening of the rose?
Through this dread shape the suffering ages look;
Time's tragedy is in that aching stoop;
Through this dread shape humanity betrayed,
Plundered, profaned and disinherited,   30
Cries protest to the Powers that made the world,
A protest that is also prophecy.

"The Man with the Hoe" reprinted by permission of Mr. Virgil Markham.

L'Estaque by Cézanne. 1883–85. Oil on Canvas. 23⅞" × 27¾". Collection, The Museum of Modern Art, New York. Gift of William S. Paley.

O masters, lords and rulers in all lands,
Is this the handiwork you give to God,
This monstrous thing distorted and soul-quencht?   35
How will you ever straighten up this shape;
Touch it again with immortality;
Give back the upward looking and the light;
Rebuild in it the music and the dream;
Make right the immemorial infamies,   40
Perfidious wrongs, immedicable woes?

O masters, lords and rulers in all lands,
How will the future reckon with this Man?
How answer his brute question in that hour
When whirlwinds of rebellion shake all shores?   45
How will it be with kingdoms and with kings—
With those who shaped him to the thing he is—
When this dumb Terror shall rise to judge the world,
After the silence of the centuries?

Cézanne's Ports

Allen Ginsberg (1926–   )

In the foreground we see time and life
swept in a race
toward the left hand side of the picture
where shore meets shore.

But that meeting place   5
isn't represented;
it doesn't occur on the canvas.

For the other side of the bay
is Heaven and Eternity,
with a bleak white haze over its mountains.   10

And the immense water of L'Estaque is a go-between
for minute rowboats.

L'Estaque (l. 11): a fishing village near Marseilles, France. It is the title of Cezanne's painting.

"Cézanne's Ports" reprinted with permission of Corinth Books.

Matisse: "The Red Studio"

W. D. Snodgrass (1926–   )

There is no one here.
But the objects: they are real. It is not
As if he had stepped out or moved away;
There is no other room and no
Returning. Your foot or finger would pass   5
Through, as into unreflecting water
Red with clay, or into fire.
Still, the objects: they are real. It is
As if he had stood
Still in the bare center of this floor,   10
His mind turned in in concentrated fury,
Till he sank
Like a great beast sinking into sands
Slowly, and did not look up.
His own room drank him.   15
What else could generate this
Terra cotta raging through the floor and walls,
Through chests, chairs, the table and the clock,
Till all environments of living are
Transformed to energy—   20
Crude, definitive and gay.
And so gave birth to objects that are real.
How slowly they took shape, his children, here,
Grew solid and remain:
The crayons; these statues; the clear brandybowl;   25
The ashtray where a girl sleeps, curling among flowers;
This flask of tall glass, green, where a vine begins
Whose bines circle the other girl brown as a cypress knee.
Then, pictures, emerging on the walls:
Bathers; a landscape; a still life with a vase;   30
To the left, a golden blonde, lain in magentas with flowers scattering like stars;
Opposite, top right, these terra cotta women, living, in their world of
       living's colors;
Between, but yearning toward them, the sailor on his red café chair, dark
       blue, self-absorbed.
These stay, exact,
Within the belly of these walls that burn,   35
That must hum like the domed electric web
Within which, at the carnival, small cars bump and turn,
Toward which, for strength, they reach their iron hands:
Like the heavens' walls of flame that the old magi could see;

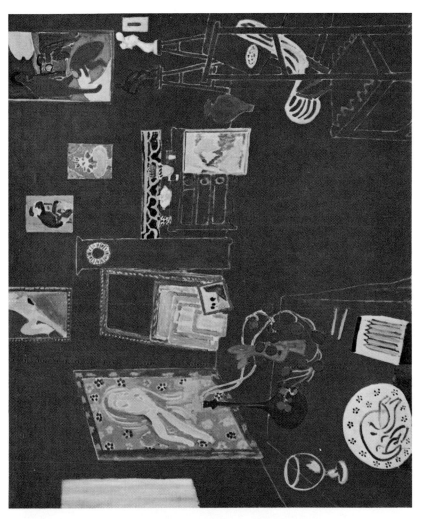

The Red Studio by Matisse. 1911. Oil on canvas. 71¼″ × 86¼″. Collection, The Museum of Modern Art, New York. Mrs. Simon Guggenheim Fund.

Nude Descending a Staircase, No. 2 by Duchamp. 1912. Oil on canvas. 58" × 35". Phila-delphia Museum of Art. The Louise and Walter Arensberg Collection.

Or those ethereal clouds of energy   40
From which all constellations form,
Within whose love they turn.
They stand here real and ultimate.
But there is no one here.

Nude Descending a Staircase

X. J. Kennedy (1929–   )

Toe upon toe, a snowing flesh,
A gold of lemon, root and rind,
She sifts in sunlight down the stairs
With nothing on. Nor on her mind.

We spy beneath the banister   5
A constant thresh of thigh on thigh—
Her lips imprint the swinging air
That parts to let her parts go by.

One-woman waterfall, she wears
Her slow descent like a long cape   10
And pausing, on the final stair
Collects her motions into shape.

City Square by Giacometti. 1948. Bronze. 8½" × 25⅜" × 17¼". Collection, The Museum of Modern Art, New York. Purchased.

The Tall Figures of Giacometti

May Swenson (1919–   )

We move by means of our mud bumps.
We bubble as do the dead but more slowly.

The products of excruciating purges
we are squeezed out thin hard and dry.

If we exude a stench it is petrified sainthood.   5
Our feet are large crude fused together

solid like anvils. Ugly as truth is ugly
we are meant to stand upright a long time

and shudder without motion
under the scintillating pins of light   10

that dart between our bodies
of pimpled mud and your eyes.

155

Number 1 by Jackson Pollock (1948)

Nancy Sullivan (1929–   )

No name but a number.
Trickles and valleys of paint
Devise this maze
Into a game of Monopoly
Without any bank. Into   5
A linoleum on the floor
In a dream. Into
Murals inside of the mind.
No similes here. Nothing
But paint. Such purity   10
Taxes the poem that speaks
Still of something in a place
Or at a time.
How to realize his question
Let alone his answer?   15

"Number 1 by Jackson Pollock (1948)" from *Ramparts* reprinted by permission of Nancy Sullivan.

Number 1 by Jackson Pollock. 1948. Oil on canvas. 68″ × 104″. Collection, The Museum of Modern Art, New York. Purchase.

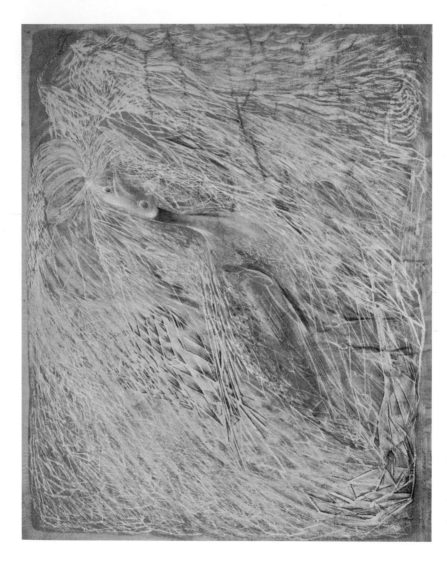

Bird in the Spirit by Morris Graves. 1943. Tempera on paper. 24″ × 30″. Metropolitan Museum of Art, Arthur H. Hearn Funds, 1950.

[The wounded wilderness of Morris Graves]

Lawrence Ferlinghetti (1919–   )

The wounded wilderness of Morris Graves
   is not the same wild west
               the white man found
It is a land that Buddha came upon
               from a different direction   5
   It is a wild white nest
         in the true mad north
                  of introspection
     where 'falcons of the inner eye'
                dive and die   10
       glimpsing in their dying fall
            all life's memory
              of existence
     and with grave chalk wing
            draw upon the leaded sky   15
a thousand threaded images
         of flight

It is the night that is their 'native habitat'
   these 'spirit birds' with bled white wings
     these droves of plover   20
        bearded eagles
         blind birds singing
           in glass fields
these moonmad swans and ecstatic ganders
                 trapped egrets   25
         charcoal owls
            trotting turtle symbols
these pink fish among mountains
        shrikes seeking to nest
     whitebone drones   30
        mating in air
    among hallucinary moons

And a masked bird fishing
       in a golden stream
and an ibis feeding   35
     'on its own breast'
  and a stray Connemara Pooka
       (life size)

And then those blown mute birds
                            bearing fish and paper messages   40
            between two streams
                        which are the twin streams
                                        of oblivion
                wherein the imagination
                                turning upon itself   45
                with white electric vision
                                refinds itself still mad
                        and unfed
                                among the hebrides

Six

Poetry, Sound, and Music

Each of the arts works in its own way. Though we may use the same terms in dealing with different art forms, the meanings of our terms may not carry over from one form to the other: clearly the "movement" of a poem is something different from the "movement" of a dance. And some terms do not carry over at all: poetry can employ didacticism or paradox but music cannot. The medium of poetry is language, and inseparable from language is meaning. Words refer to things and concepts and feelings.

We needn't plunge into a philosophical discussion of the meaning of meaning, however, to recognize that the meaning of poetry involves much more than the dictionary definitions of words. The dictionary will be of little help in our attempting to understand the meaning of rhyme, rhythm, meter, or alliteration in a particular poem. Yeats tells us in "Adam's Curse" that the job of the poet is "to articulate sweet sounds together." The meaning of these words (including the metaphoric use of "sweet") poses no particular problem, though we would probably find it difficult to explain the pleasing effect of the alliteration in "sweet sounds."

The alliteration is, in a sense, the musical equivalent of the meaning of the words, an example of sound supporting sense. Although the music of a poem is undoubtedly felt when one reads silently, it is given fuller play when the poem is read aloud. A printed poem is static and unchanging. Read aloud, it takes on new meanings. And when recited by different readers, the same poem reveals its range of possible interpretations. Alliteration, assonance, consonance, as well as tempo, emphasis, pauses—even pitch and tone—all contribute to our understanding of the poem. In other words, the reading of a poem is a kind of secondary creative act, for the reader creates one of the many possible interpretations inherent in the printed work. Read badly, the sweet sounds of the poem may turn sour; read sensitively, the sweet sounds are music.

When Robert Frost said that "Poetry is that which is lost in translation," he was, in pointing out the nuances of meaning that individual words carry, also reminding us of how important the music of poetry is. Paradoxically, it is this important aspect of poetry that is often the most difficult to identify and account for. The traditional vocabulary of poetic analysis includes many terms, some of them already referred to above, that identify musical effects. These terms provide a basic and indispensable means of beginning to discuss musical effects.

This chapter is devoted to joining sounds to words. It includes works that have been recorded in readings by the poets, traditional ballads that have been set to music by modern artists, as well as modern rock or pop songs. As poems, you will want to bring to them the same approaches and techniques of analysis you have developed thus far. But the opportunity to hear poems read or sung with instrumental accompaniment will open up new kinds of questions and considerations. Does hearing a poem read by the author give you new insights or enhance your appreciation of the work? Or, conversely, do you feel that the poet has failed to read his poem effectively? Do some of the poems strike you as successful in song but weak and thin as poetry? Or, put another way, do words, when sung to instrumental accompaniment, tend to become assimilated by the music and thereby take on a richness of effect they do not have on the printed page?

These are questions that will be worth discussing as you read and listen to the poems included in this chapter. But remember: it is much easier to formulate questions about poetry and music than to answer them. We are all powerfully moved by music but feel powerless (or nearly so) to explain why. Yet asking questions in itself can be a form of clarification and discovery. Let us, finally, also remember that poetry, in T. S. Eliot's words, "can communicate without being understood."

Lord Randall

Traditional

O where have you been, Lord Randall, my son?
Tell me where have you been, my handsome young one?
I've been with my sweetheart, mother,
I've been with my sweetheart, mother
O, make my bed soon for I'm sick to the heart   5
And I fain would lie doon.

And what did she give you for supper, Lord Randall, my son?
What'd she give you for supper, my handsome young one?
Eels and eel broth, mother,
Ay, eels and eel broth, mother.   10
Make my bed soon for I'm sick to the heart and I fain would lie doon.

And what color were the skins, Lord Randall, my son?
And what color were the skins, my handsome young one?
All brown and speckled, mother
All brown and speckled, mother   15
Make my bed soon for I'm sick to the heart and I fain would lie doon.

I have fear you been poisoned, Lord Randall, my son.
I have fear you been poisoned, my handsome young one.
O yes, and I'm dead, mother
O yes, and I'm dead, mother.   20
Make my bed soon for I'm sick to the heart and I fain would lie doon.

What bequeath ye your mother, Lord Randall, my son?
What bequeath ye your mother, my handsome young one?
My gold and silver, mother,
All my gold and silver, mother.   25
Make my bed soon for I'm sick to the heart and I fain would lie doon.

What bequeath ye your sweetheart, Lord Randall, my son?
What bequeath ye your sweetheart, my handsome young one?
A rope from hell to hang her,
Bring a rope from hell to hang her.   30
Make my bed soon for I'm sick to the heart and I fain would lie doon.

Sung by Buffy Sainte-Marie, *Fire and Fleet and Candlelight* (Vanguard VRS-9250).

The House Carpenter

Traditional

Well met, well met, my own true love,
Well met, well met, cried he,
I've just returned from the salt, salt sea,
All for the love of thee.

This version of "The House Carpenter" is used by permission of Vanguard Recording Soc.,
Inc.

163

I could have married the king's daughter, dear,   5
She would have married me,
But I have forsaken the crowns of gold,
All for the love of thee.

Well, if you could have married the king's daughter, dear,
I'm sure you are to blame,   10
For I am married to a house carpenter,
Find him a nice young man.

Ah, will you forsake your house carpenter,
And go along with me,
I'll take you to where the grass grows green,   15
The banks of the salt, salt sea?

Well, if I should forsake my house carpenter,
And go along with thee,
What have you got to maintain me on,
And keep me from poverty?   20

Six ships, six ships, all upon the sea,
Seven more upon dry land,
One hundred and ten all brave sailing men,
The sea is your command.

She picked up her own wee babe,   25
Kisses gave him three,
Stay right here with my house carpenter,
Keep him good company.

And she put on her rich attire,
So glorious to behold,   30
And as she trod along her way,
She shone like the glittering gold.

Well, they'd not been gone but about two weeks,
I know it was not three,
And this fair lady began to weep,   35
She wept most bitterly,

Ah, why do you weep my fair young maid,
Weepest for your golden store,
Or do you weep for your house carpenter,
Never you shall see anymore.   40

I do not weep for my house carpenter,
Or for any golden store,

164

I do weep for my own wee babe,
Never you shall see anymore?

Well, they'd not been gone but about three weeks,   45
I'm sure it was not four,
Our gallant ship sprang a leak and sank,
Never to rise anymore.

One time around spun our gallant ship,
Two times around spun she,   50
Three times around spun our gallant ship,
And sank to the bottom of the sea.

What hills, what hills are those my love?
And why so fair and high?
Those are the hills of heaven my love,   55
And they aren't for you and I.

And what hills, what hills are those, my love?
Those hills so bold and low?
Those are the hills of hell, my love,
Where you and I must go.   60

Sung by Joan Baez, *Joan Baez in Concert* (Vanguard, VRS-9112).

Barbara Allen

Traditional

In Scarlet Town, where I was born
There was a fair maid dwellin'
Made many a youth cry well-a-day
And her name was Barbry Allen.

'Twas in the merry month of May   5
When green buds, they were swellin'.
Sweet William came from the west country
And he courted Barbry Allen.

He sent his servant unto her
To the place where she was dwellin'.   10
"My master's sick, bids me call for you
If your name be Barbry Allen."

This version of "Barbara Allen" is used by permission of Vanguard Recording Soc., Inc.

Well slowly, slowly got she up
And slowly went she nigh him,
But all she said as she passed his bed,   15
"Young man I think you're dyin'."

He turned his pale face to the wall
And busted out a cryin',
Adieu, adieu, my dear friends all
Be kind to Barbry Allen.   20

Well lightly tripped she down the stair
She heard those church bells tollin'
And each bell seemed to say as it tolled
Hard hearted Barbry Allen.

And she looked east and she looked west   25
She seen his pale corpse a-comin',
Lay down, lay down that corpse of clay
That I may look upon him.

O mother, mother, go make my bed.
Go make it long and narrow,   30
Sweet William died for me today
I'll die for him tomorrow.

They buried Sweet William in the old churchyard.
They buried Barbara beside him,
Out of his grave grew a red, red rose,   35
And out of hers a briar.

They grew and grew up the old church wall
Till they could grow no higher
And at the top, twined in a lover's knot
A red rose and the briar.   40

Sung by Joan Baez, *Vol. II* (Vanguard VRS-9094).

166

The Unquiet Grave

Traditional

"Cold blows the wind to my true-love,
And gently drops the rain;
I never had but one true-love
And in Greenwood he lies slain."

"I'll do as much for my true-love   5
An any young girl may;
I'll sit and moan all on his grave,
For a twelvemonths and a day."

And when twelvemonths and a day was past
The ghost did rise and speak: 10
"Why sittest thou all on my grave
And will not let me sleep?"

"Go fetch me water from the desert
And blood from out of a stone.
Go fetch me milk from a fair maid's breast   15
That a young man never has known."

"How oft' in yonder grove, Sweetheart
Where we were wont to walk,
The finest flower that ere I saw
Has withered to a stalk."   20

"The stalk is withered and dead, Sweetheart,
The flower will never return.
And since I lost my own true-love
What can I do but yearn?"

"When will we meet again, Sweetheart,   25
When will we meet again?"
"When the autumn leaves that fall from the trees
Are green and spring up again."

Sung by Joan Baez, "#5", (Vanguard VSD-79160).

This version of "The Unquiet Grave" is used by permission of Vanguard Recording Soc., Inc.

167

Swing Low, Sweet Chariot

Traditional Negro Spiritual

Swing low, sweet chariot,
Comin' for to carry me home,
Swing low, sweet chariot,
Comin' for to carry me home.

I looked over Jordan and what did I see,   5
Comin' for to carry me home,
A band of angels, comin' after me,
Comin' for to carry me home.

If you get there before I do,
Comin' for to carry me home,   10
Tell all my friends I'm comin' too,
Comin' for to carry me home.

Swing low, sweet chariot,
Comin' for to carry me home,
Swing low, sweet chariot,   15
Comin' for to carry me home.

Sung by Paul Robeson, *Robeson in Live Performance* (Columbia M-30424); Leontyne
Price, *Swing Low, Sweet Chariot* (Columbia, Victor LSC-2600); Big Maybelle, *Gospel
Soul of Big Maybelle* (Brunswick 754142); Norman Luboff Choir, *Songs of the South* (Colum-
bia CS-9045); Singing Churchman, *What Wondrous Love* (Word 8356).

Sometimes I Feel like a Motherless Child

Traditional Negro Spiritual

Sometimes I feel like a motherless child,
Sometimes I feel like a motherless child,
Sometimes I feel like a motherless child,
A long ways from home, a long ways from home.

Come my brother, a long ways from home,   5
A long ways from home.

Sometimes I feel like I'm almos' gone,
Sometimes I feel like I'm almos' gone,
Sometimes I feel like I'm almos' gone,
A long ways from home, a long ways from home.   10

Come my sister, a long ways from home,
A long ways from home.

Sung by Paul Robeson, *Robeson* (Vanguard 2015); Marian Anderson, *He's Got the Whole World in His Hands* (Victor LSC-2592); Mahalia Jackson, *Bless This House* (Columbia CS-8761); Odetta, *Odetta at Carnegie Hall* (Vanguard 2072); Peter, Paul and Mary, *Song Will Rise* (Warner Bros. 1589).

'Zekiel Saw the Wheel

Traditional Negro Spiritual

Wheel, oh wheel,
Wheel in the middle of a wheel,
Wheel, oh wheel,
Wheel in the middle of a wheel.

'Zekiel saw the wheel of time,   5
Wheel in the middle of a wheel,
Every spoke was human kind,
Wheel in the middle of a wheel.

Way up yonder on the mountain,
Wheel in the middle of a wheel,   10
My Lord spoke and the chariot stop,
Wheel in the middle of a wheel.

'Zekiel saw the wheel,
Way up in the middle of the air,
'Zekiel saw the wheel,   15
Way up in the middle of the air.

The big wheel run by faith,
Little wheel run by the grace of God,
Wheel within a wheel,
Way in the middle of the air.   20

Oh the big wheel run by faith
Little wheel run by the grace of God,
Wheel within wheel,
Way in the middle of the air.

169

Wheel, oh wheel,   25
Wheel in the middle of a wheel,
Wheel, oh wheel,
Wheel in the middle of a wheel.

See Ezekiel, 1:15–28; 3:13; 10:9–22.

Sung by Paul Robeson, *Robeson in Live Performance* (Columbia M-30424); Harry Bela-
fonte, *My Lord, What a Mornin'* (Victor LSP-2022); Woody Guthrie, *Early Years* (Tradition
2088); Cisco Houston, *Cisco Houston* (Everest 205); Rooftop Singers, *Rain River* (Van-
guard 79190).

Didn't My Lord Deliver Daniel?

Traditional Negro Spiritual

Didn't my Lord deliver Daniel,
Deliver Daniel,
Deliver Daniel,
Didn't my Lord deliver Daniel,
And why not every man?   5

He delivered Daniel from the lion's den
Jonah from the belly of the whale
And the Hebrew children from the fiery furnace,
And why not every man?

Didn't my Lord deliver Daniel,   10
Deliver Daniel,
Deliver Daniel,
Didn't my Lord deliver Daniel,
And why not every man?

The moon run down in a purple stream,   15
The sun refused to shine,
Every star it disappear,
Yes, Jesus shall be mine.

Didn't my Lord deliver Daniel,
Deliver Daniel,   20
Deliver Daniel,
Didn't my Lord deliver Daniel,
And why not every man?

See Daniel, 6.

Sung by Paul Robeson, *Paul Robeson at Carnegie Hall* (Vanguard 2035); Robert Shaw
Chorale, *Deep River* (Victor LSC-2247), *Sing Out, Sweet Land* (Decca 74304).

John Henry

Traditional Negro Ballad

John Henry was a little baby,
Sittin' on his mammy's knee,
Said, "The Big Bend tunnel on the C. & O. road
Gonna be the death of me,
Lawd, Lawd, gonna be the death of me."   5

John Henry was a little baby,
Sittin' on his daddy's knee,
Point his finger at a little piece of steel,
"That's gonna be the death of me,
Lawd, Lawd, that's gonna be the death of me."   10

John Henry had a little woman
And her name was Mary Magdelene,
She would go to the tunnel and sing for John
Jes' to hear John Henry's hammer ring,
Lawd, Lawd, jes' to hear John Henry's hammer ring.   15

John Henry had a little woman
And her name was Polly Anne,
John Henry took sick and he had to go to bed,
Polly Anne drove steel like a man,
Lawd, Lawd, Polly Anne drove steel like a man.   20

Cap'n says to John Henry,
"Gonna bring me a steam drill 'round,
Gonna take that steam drill out on the job,
Gonna whop that steel on down,
Lawd, Lawd, gonna whop that steel on down."   25

John Henry told his cap'n,
Said, "A man ain't nothin' but a man,
And befo' I'd let that steam drill beat me down
I'd die with this hammer in my hand,
Lawd, Lawd, I'd die with the hammer in my hand."   30

Sun were hot and burnin',
Weren't no breeze atall,
Sweat ran down like water down a hill,
That day John let his hammer fall,
Lawd, Lawd, that day John let his hammer fall.   35

White man told John Henry,
"Nigger, damn yo' soul,
You may beat dis steam and drill of mine,—
When the rocks in the mountains turn to gold,
Lawd, Lawd, when the rocks in the mountains turn to gold."   40

John Henry said to his shaker,
"Shaker, why don't you sing?
I'm throwin' twelve pounds from my hips on down,
Jes' lissen to the cold steel ring,
Lawd, Lawd, jes' lissen to the cold steel ring."   45

O the cap'n told John Henry,
"I b'lieve this mountain's sinkin' in,"
John Henry said to his cap'n, "O my,
It's my hammer just a-hossin' in the wind,
Lawd, Lawd, it's my hammer just a-hossin' in the wind."   50

John Henry told his shaker,
"Shaker, you better pray,
For, if I miss this six-foot steel
Tomorrow be yo' buryin' day,
Lawd, Lawd, tomorrow be yo' buryin' day."   55

John Henry told his captain,
"Looky yonder what I see—
Yo' drill's done broke an' yo' hole's done choke,
An' you can't drive steel like me,
Lawd, Lawd, an' you can't drive steel like me."   60

John Henry was hammerin' on the mountain,
An' his hammer was strikin' fire,
He drove so hard till he broke his pore heart
An' he lied down his hammer an' he died,
Lawd, Lawd, he lied down his hammer an' he died.   65

They took John Henry to the graveyard
An' they buried him in the sand
An' ev'ry locomotive come roarin' by,
Says, "There lays a steel drivin' man,"
Lawd, Lawd, "There lays a steel drivin' man."   70

Legendary hero of many Negro ballads and tales. There are scores of versions of this poem.

Sung by Sonny Terry and Brownie McGhee, *Shouts and Blues* (Fantasy 3317); Big Bill Broonzy, *Big Bill Broonzy Sings Folk Songs* (Fantasy FA 2328); Furry Lewis, *Back on My Feet Again* (Prestige 7810); Odetta and Larry, *Odetta* (Fantasy 8345); Pete Seeger, *Freight Train* (Capitol DT-2718); Josh White, *Best of Josh White* (Elektra 75008); Woody Guthrie, *Legendary Woody Guthrie* (Everest 204); Harry Belafonte, *Harry Belafonte at Carnegie Hall* (Victor LSO-6006).

Follow the Drinkin' Gourd

Traditional Negro Folk Song

Follow the drinkin' gourd,
Follow the drinkin' gourd,
For the old man is a-waitin' for to carry you to freedom,
Follow the drinkin' gourd.

When the sun comes back, and the first quail calls,   5
Follow the drinkin' gourd,
When the old man is a-waitin' for to carry you to freedom,
Follow the drinkin' gourd.

Follow the drinkin' gourd,
Follow the drinkin' gourd,   10
For the old man is a-waitin' for to carry you to freedom,
Follow the drinkin' gourd.

Well, the river bank will make a mighty good road,
The dead trees will show you the way,
Left foot, big foot, travelin' on,   15
Follow the drinkin' gourd.

Follow the drinkin' gourd,
Follow the drinkin' gourd,
For the old man is a-waitin' for to carry you to freedom,
Follow the drinkin' gourd.   20

Well, the river ends between two hills,
Follow the drinkin' gourd,
There's another river on the other side,
Follow the drinkin' gourd.

Follow the drinkin' gourd,   25
Follow the drinkin' gourd,
For the old man is a-waitin' for to carry you to freedom,
Follow the drinkin' gourd.

A slave song. The "drinkin' gourd" referred to the Big Dipper, which led northward to freedom.

Sung by Pete Seeger, *I Can See a New Day* (Columbia CS-9057); Theodore Bikel, *From Bondage to Freedom* (Elektra EKS-7200).

When That I Was a Tiny Little Boy

William Shakespeare (1564–1616)

When that I was and a little tiny boy,
   With hey, ho, the wind and the rain,
A foolish thing was but a toy,
   For the rain it raineth every day.

But when I came to man's estate,   5
   With hey, ho, the wind and the rain,
'Gainst knaves and thieves men shut their gate,
   For the rain it raineth every day.

But when I came, alas! to wive,
   With hey, ho, the wind and the rain,   10
By swaggering could I never thrive,
   For the rain it raineth every day.

But when I came unto my beds,
   With hey, ho, the wind and the rain,
With toss-pots still had drunken heads,   15
   For the rain it raineth every day.

A great while ago the world begun,
   With hey, ho, the wind and the rain;
But that's all one, our play is done,
   And we'll strive to please you every day.   20

Recorded on *Songs from the Plays of Shakespeare* (Caedmon SRS 242-M).

Heart's Ease

William Shakespeare (1564–1616)

Sing care away, with sport and play,
   For pastime is our pleasure;
If well we fare, for nought we care,
   In mirth consists our treasure.

Let stupids lurk, and drudges work,   5
   We do defy their slav'ry;
He is a fool that goes to school,
   All we delight in brav'ry.

What doth avail far hence to sail,
   And lead our life in toiling?   10
Or to what end should we here spend,
   Our days in irksome moiling?

It is the best to live at rest,
   And tak't as God doth send it,
To haunt each wake and mirth to make,   15
   And with good fellows spend it.

Recorded on *Songs from the Plays of Shakespeare* (Caedmon SRS 242-M).

Tomorrow Is St. Valentine's Day

William Shakespeare (1564–1616)

Tomorrow is Saint Valentine's day,
   All in the morning betime,
And I a maid at your window,
   To be your valentine.

Then up he rose and donned his clothes   5
   And dupped the chamber door,
Let in the maid, that out a maid
   Never departed more.

By Gis and by Saint Charity,
   Alack and fie for shame!   10
Young men will do't if they come to't;
   By Cock, they are to blame.
Quoth she, before you tumbled me,
   You promis'd me to wed.
So would I ha' done by yonder sun,   15
   And thou hadst not come to my bed.

dupped (l. 6): opened.   *Gis* (l. 9): Jesus

Recorded on *Songs from the Plays of Shakespeare* (Caedmon SRS 242-M).

Full Fathom Five

William Shakespeare (1564–1616)

Full fathom five thy father lies,
   Of his bones are coral made:
Those are pearls that were his eyes;
   Nothing of him that doth fade
But doth suffer a sea-change   5
Into something rich and strange.
Sea nymphs hourly ring his knell:
        Ding, dong.
Hark, now I hear them: ding-dong bell.

Recorded on *Songs from the Plays of Shakespeare* (Caedmon SRS 242-M).

Sing We and Chant It

Thomas Morley (1557–1603?)

Sing we and chant it,
While love doth grant it, falala.
Not long youth lasteth,
And old age hasteth,
Now is best leisure   5
To take our pleasure, falala.

All things invite us,
Now to delight us, falala.
Hence, care, be packing,
No mirth be lacking,   10
Let spare no treasure
To live in pleasure, falala.

Sung on *Renaissance Vocal Music* (Nonesuch H-1097).

The Sound of Silence

Paul Simon (1942–   )

Hello darkness my old friend,
I've come to talk with you again,
Because a vision softly creeping,
Left its seeds while I was sleeping
And the vision that was planted in my brain   5
Still remains within the sound of silence.

In restless dreams I walked alone,
Narrow streets of cobble stone
'Neath the halo of a street lamp,
I turned my collar to the cold and damp   10
When my eyes were stabbed by the flash of a neon light
That split the night, and touched the sound of silence.

And in the naked light I saw
Ten thousand people maybe more,
People talking without speaking,   15
People hearing without listening,
People writing songs that voices never share
And no one dares disturb the sound of silence.

"Fools!" said I, "You do not know
Silence like a cancer grows.   20
Hear my words that I might teach you,
Take my arms that I might reach you."
But my words like silent raindrops fell
And echoed, in the wells of silence.

And the people bowed and prayed   25
To the neon God they made,
And the sign flashed out its warning
In the words that it was forming,
And the sign said:
    "The words of the prophets are written
    on the subway walls and tenement halls"   30
And whispered in the sound of silence.

Sung by Simon and Garfunkel, *Sounds of Silence* (Columbia CS-9269).

Desolation Row

Bob Dylan (1941–   )

They're selling postcards of the hanging
They're painting the passports brown
The beauty parlor's filled with sailors
The circus is in town
Here comes the blind commissioner   5
They've got him in a trance
One hand's tied to the tight-rope walker
The other is in his pants
And the riot squad they're restless
They need somewhere to go   10
As lady and I look out tonight
From Desolation Row.

Cinderella she seems so easy
It takes one to know one she smiles
Then puts her hands in her back pocket   15
Bette Davis style
Then in comes Romeo he's moaning
You belong to me I believe
Then someone says you're in the wrong place my friend
You'd better leave   20
And the only sound that's left
After the ambulances go
Is Cinderella sweeping up
On Desolation Row.

Now Ophelia she's 'neath the window   25
For her I feel so afraid
On her twenty second birthday
She already is an old maid
To her death is quite romantic
She wears an iron vest   30
Her profession's her religion
Her sin is her lifelessness
And though her eyes are fixed upon
Noah's great rainbow
She spends her time peeking   35
Into Desolation Row.

Doctor filth he keeps his word
Inside of a leather cup
But all his sexless patients
They're trying to blow it up   40
Now his nurse some local loser
She's in charge of the cyanide hole
And she also keeps the cards that read
Have mercy on his soul
They all play on penny whistles   45
You can hear them blow
If you lean your head out far enough
From Desolation Row.

Now at midnight all the agents
And the super human crew   50
Come out and round up everyone
That knows more than they do
Then they bring them to the factory
Where the heart attack machine
Is strapped across their shoulders   55
And then the kerosene
Is brought down from the castles
By insurance men who go
Check to see that nobody is escaping
To Desolation Row.   60

Now the moon is almost hidden
The stars are beginning to hide
The fortune telling lady
Has even taken all her things inside
All except for Cain and Abel   65
And the hunchback of Notre Dame
Everybody is making love
Or else expecting rain
And the good samaritan he's dressing
He's getting ready for the show   70
He's going to the carnival
Tonight on Desolation Row.

Einstein disguised as Robin Hood
With his memories in a trunk
Passed this way an hour ago   75
With his friend a jealous monk
He looked so immaculately frightful
As he bummed a cigarette
Then he went off sniffing drain pipes
And reciting the alphabet   80

179

Now you would not think to look at him
But he was famous long ago
For playing the electric violin
On Desolation Row.

Across the street they've nailed the curtains   85
They're getting ready for the feast
The phantom of the opera
A perfect image of a priest
They're spoon feeding Casanova
To get him to feel more assured   ·90
Then they'll kill him with self confidence
After poisoning him with words
And the phantom shouting to skinny girls
Get outta here if you don't know
Casanova is just being punished   95
For going to Desolation Row.

Praise be to Nero's Neptune
The Titanic sails at dawn
And everybody's shouting
Which side are you on?   100
And Ezra Pound and T. S. Eliot
Fighting in the captain's tower
While calypso singers laugh at them
And fishermen hold flowers
Between the windows of the sea   105
Where lovely mermaids flow
And nobody has to think too much
About Desolation Row.

Yes I received your letter yesterday
About the time the door knob broke   110
When you asked how I was doing
Was that some kind of joke
All these people that you mentioned
Yes I know them they're quite lame
I had to rearrange their faces   115
And give them all another name
Right now I can't read too good
Don't send me no more letters no
Not unless you mail them from
Desolation Row.   120

Sung by Bob Dylan, *Highway 61 Revisited* (Columbia CS-9189).

180

The Song of Wandering Aengus

W. B. Yeats (1865–1939)

I went out to the hazel wood,
Because a fire was in my head,
And cut and peeled a hazel wand,
And hooked a berry to a thread;
And when white moths were on the wing,   5
And moth-like stars were flickering out,
I dropped the berry in a stream
And caught a little silver trout.

When I had laid it on the floor
I went to blow the fire aflame,   10
But something rustled on the floor,
And someone called my by my name:
It had become a glimmering girl
With apple blossom in her hair
Who called me by my name and ran   15
And faded through the brightening air.

Though I am old with wandering
Through hollow lands and hilly lands,
I will find out where she has gone,
And kiss her lips and take her hands;   20
And walk among long dappled grass,
And pluck till time and times are done
The silver apples of the moon,
The golden apples of the sun.

Sung by Judy Collins, *The Golden Apples of the Sun* (Elektra EKS-7222).

Fire and Rain

James Taylor (1948–   )

Just yesterday morning they let me know you were gone,
Susan the plans they made put an end to you.
I walked out this morning and I wrote down this song,
I just can't remember who to send it to.

I've seen fire and I've seen rain,   5
I've seen sunny days that I thought would never end,
I've seen lonely times when I could not find a friend,
But I always thought that I'd see you again.

Won't you look down upon me Jesus, you gotta help me make a stand,
Just gotta see me through another day.   10
My body's aching and my time is at hand,
I won't make it any other way.

I've seen fire and I've seen rain,
I've seen sunny days that I thought would never end,
I've seen lonely times when I could not find a friend,   15
But I always thought that I'd see you again.

I've been walking my mind to an easy time, my back turned towards
        the sun,
Lord knows when the cold wind blows it'll turn your head around.
Well, there's hours of time on the telephone line to talk about things
        to come,
Sweet dreams and flying machines in pieces on the ground.   20

I've seen fire and I've seen rain,
I've seen sunny days that I thought would never end,
I've seen lonely times when I could not find a friend,
But I always thought that I'd see you again.

Thought I'd see you one more time again,   25
There's just a few things coming my way this time around,
Thought I'd see you, thought I'd see you. . . .

Sung by James Taylor, *Sweet Baby James* (Warner Bros. 1843). Also available on *Blood, Sweat and Tears* (Columbia KC-30090).

Suzanne

Leonard Cohen (1934–   )

Suzanne takes you down
To her place near the river.
You can hear the boats go by,
You can stay the night beside her,
And you know that she's half-crazy   5
But that's why you want to be there,
And she feeds you tea and oranges
That come all the way from China,
And just when you mean to tell her
That you have no love to give her,   10
Then she gets you on her wave-length
And she lets the river answer
That you've always been her lover.

And you want to travel with her,
And you want to travel blind,   15
And you know that she can trust you
'Cause you've touched her perfect body
With your mind.

And Jesus was a sailor
When he walked upon the water   20
And he spent a long time watching
From a lonely wooden tower
And when he knew for certain
That only drowning men could see him,
He said, "All men shall be sailors, then,   25
Until the sea shall free them,"
But he, himself, was broken
Long before the sky would open.
Forsaken, almost human,
He sank beneath your wisdom   30
Like a stone.

And you want to travel with him,
And you want to travel blind,
And you think you'll maybe trust him
'Cause he touched your perfect body   35
With his mind.

Suzanne takes your hand
And she leads you to the river.
She is wearing rags and feathers
From Salvation Army counters,   40
And the sun pours down like honey
On our lady of the harbor;
And she shows you where to look
Among the garbage and the flowers.
There are heroes in the seaweed,   45
There are children in the morning,
They are leaning out for love,
And they will lean that way forever
While Suzanne, she holds the mirror.

And you want to travel with her,   50
You want to travel blind,
And you're sure that she can find you
'Cause she's touched her perfect body
With her mind.

Sung by Leonard Cohen, *Leonard Cohen* (Columbia CS-9533). Also available on Judy Collins, *In My Life* (Elektra 74027); Nina Simone, *To Love Somebody* (Victor LSP-4152); Harry Belafonte, *Homeward Bound* (Victor LSP-4255).

A Day in the Life

John Lennon (1942–   ) and Paul McCartney (1940–   )

I read the news today, oh boy,
About a lucky man who made the grade
And though the news was rather sad
Well I just had to laugh
I saw the photograph.   5
He blew his mind out in a car
He didn't notice that the lights had changed
A crowd of people stood and stared
They'd seen his face before
Nobody was really sure   10
If he was from the House of Lords.

184

I saw a film today, oh boy,
The English army had just won the war
A crowd of people turned away
But I just had to look   15
Having read the book.
I'd love to turn you on.

Woke up, fell out of bed,
Dragged a comb across my head
Found my way downstairs and drank a cup,   20
And looking up I noticed I was late.
Found my coat and grabbed my hat
Made the bus in seconds flat
Found my way upstairs and had a smoke,
Somebody spoke and I went into a dream.   25

I read the news today, oh boy,
Four thousand holes in Blackburn,
Lancashire
And though the holes were rather small
They had to count them all   30
Now they know how many holes it takes to fill the Albert Hall.
I'd love to turn you on.

Sung by The Beatles, *Sergeant Pepper's Lonely Hearts Club Band* (Capitol SMAS-2653).

Eleanor Rigby

John Lennon (1942–   ) and Paul McCartney (1940–   )

Ah, look at all the lonely people!
Ah, look at all the lonely people!

Eleanor Rigby
Picks up the rice in the church where a wedding has been,
Lives in a dream,   5
Waits at the window
Wearing the face that she keeps in a jar by the door.
Who is it for?

ple,
   come from?   10
ole,
   belong?

...er McKenzie,
Writing the words of a sermon that no one will hear,
No one comes near   15
Look at him working,
Darning his socks in the night when there's nobody there.
What does he care?

All the lonely people
Where do they all come from?   20
All the lonely people
Where do they all belong?

Eleanor Rigby
Died in the church and was buried along with her name,
Nobody came.   25
Father McKenzie,
Wiping the dirt from his hands as he walks from the grave,
No one was saved.

All the lonely people,
Where do they all come from?   30
All the lonely people,
Where do they all belong?

Ah, look at all the lonely people!
Ah, look at all the lonely people!

Sung by The Beatles, *Revolver* (Capitol ST-2576). Also available on Joan Baez, *Joan* (Vanguard 79240); Aretha Franklin, *The Girl's in Love With You* (Atlantic 8248).

Chelsea Morning

Joni Mitchell (1943–   )

Woke up, it was a Chelsea morning, and the first thing that I heard
Was a song outside my window, and the traffic wrote the words
It came ringing up like Christmas bells, and rapping up like pipes and drums

"Chelsea Morning," words and music by Joni Mitchell. Copyright 1967. Reprinted by permission of the publisher, Siquomb Publishing Corp.

Oh, won't you stay
We'll put on the day   5
And we'll wear it 'till the night comes

Woke up, it was a Chelsea morning, and the first thing that I saw
Was the sun through yellow curtains, and a rainbow on the wall
Red, green and gold welcome you, crimson crystal beads to beckon

Oh, won't you stay   10
We'll put on the day
There's a sun show every second

Now the curtain opens on a portrait of today
And the streets are paved with passersby
And pigeons fly   15
And papers lie
Waiting to blow away

Woke up, it was a Chelsea morning, and the first thing that I knew
There was milk and toast and honey and a bowl of oranges, too

And the sun poured in like butterscotch and stuck to all my senses   20

Oh, won't you stay
We'll put on the day
And we'll talk in present tenses

When the curtain closes and the rainbow runs away
I will bring you incense owls by night   25
By candlelight
By jewel-light
If only you will stay
Pretty baby, won't you
Woke up, it is a Chelsea morning   30

Sung by Joni Mitchell, *Clouds* (Reprise 6341).

Michael from Mountains

Joni Mitchell (1943–   )

Michael wakes you up with sweets
He takes you up street and the rain comes down
Sidewalk markets locked up tight
And umbrellas bright on a grey background
There's oil on the puddles in taffeta patterns   5
That run down the drain
In colored arrangements
That Michael will change with a stick that he found.

Michael from mountains
Go where you will go to   10
Know that I will know you
Someday I may know you very well

Michael brings you to a park
He sings and it's dark when the clouds come by
Yellow slickers up on swings   15
Like puppets on strings hanging in the sky
They'll splash home to suppers in wallpapered kitchens
Their mothers will scold
But Michael will hold you
To keep away cold till the sidewalks are dry   20

Michael from mountains
Go where you will go to
Know that I will know you
Someday I may know you very well

Michael leads you up the stairs   25
He needs you to care and you know you do
Cats come crying to the key
And dry you will be in a towel or two
There's rain in the window
There's sun in the painting that smiles on the wall   30
You want to know all
But his mountains have called so you never do

Michael from mountains
Go where you will go to
Know that I will know you   35
Someday I may know you very well

Sung by Joni Mitchell, *Joni Mitchell* (Reprise 6293). Also available on Judy Collins, *Wild-flowers* (Elektra 74012).

My Father

Judy Collins (1939–   )

My father always promised us
    that we would live in France,
We'd go boating on the Seine
    and I would learn to dance.
We lived in Ohio then   5
    he worked in the mines,
On his streams like boats we knew
    we'd sail, in time.

All my sisters soon were gone
    to Denver and Cheyenne,   10
Marrying their grownup dreams,
    the lilacs and the man.
I stayed behind the youngest still,
    only danced alone,
The colors of my father's dreams   15
    faded without a sigh.

And I live in Paris now,
    my children dance and dream
Hearing the ways of a miner's life
    in words they've never seen.   20
I sail my memories afar
    like boats across the Seine,
And watch the Paris sun
    set in my father's eyes again.

189

My father always promised us   25
    that we would live in France,
We'd go boating on the Seine
    and I would learn to dance.
We lived in Ohio then
    he worked in the mines,   30
On his streams like boats we knew
    we'd sail, in time.

Sung by Judy Collins, *Who Knows Where the Time Goes* (Elektra 74023).

Ballad of Birmingham

Dudley Randall (1914–   )

Mother dear may I go downtown
Instead of out to play
And march the streets of Birmingham
In a freedom march today?

No baby no, you may not go   5
For the dogs are fierce and wild,
And clubs and hoses, guns and jails
Aren't good for a little child.

But mother I won't be alone,
Other children will go with me   10
And march the streets of Birmingham
To make our people free.

No baby no, you may not go
I fear the guns will fire,
But you may go to church instead and sing in the
        children's choir.   15

She's combed and brushed her night dark hair
And bathed rose petal sweet,
And drawn white gloves on small brown hands,
White shoes on her feet.

Her mother smiled to know her child   20
Was in that sacred place,
But that smile was the last
Smile to come to her face.

For when she heard the explosion
Her eyes grew wet and wild,   25
She raced through the streets of Birmingham
Yelling for her child.

She dug in bits of glass and brick,
Then pulled out a shoe
Oh here is the shoe my baby wore   30
But baby where are you?

Sung by Jerry Moore, *Jerry Moore* (ESP Disk 1061).

God Bless the Child

Arthur Herzog, Jr. (1900–   ) and Billie Holiday (1915–1959)

Them that's got shall have,
Them that's not shall lose,
So the Bible said,
And it still is news,

Mama may have   5
Papa may have
But God bless the child,
That's got his own.

Yes the strong gets more,
While the weak ones fade,   10
Empty pockets don't,
Ever make the grade,

Mama may have
Papa may have
But God bless the child,   15
That's got his own.

Money, you've got lots of friends,
They're crowdin' 'round your door,
But when you're gone and spending ends,
They don't come no more,   20

Rich relations give,
Crust of bread and such,
You can help yourself,
But don't take too much.

Mama may have   25
Papa may have
But God bless the child,
That's got his own.

He just don't worry 'bout nothin',
'Cause he's got his own,   30
Yes, he's got his own.

Sung by Billie Holiday, *Lady Sings the Blues* (Verve 6-8099); Billie Holiday, *The Billie Holiday Story* (Decca DXSB-7161); Billie Holiday, *Billie Holiday's Greatest Hits* (Columbia CL-2666). Also available on *Blood, Sweat and Tears* (Columbia CS-9720); Aretha Franklin, *Tender, Moving, Swinging Aretha Franklin* (Columbia CS-8676); Liza Minnelli, *New Feelin'* (A&M 4272); Lou Rawls and Les McCann, *Stormy Monday* (Capitol ST-1714).

Turn! Turn! Turn!

Pete Seeger (1919–   )

To everything,
Turn, turn, turn,
There is a season,
Turn, turn, turn,
And a time to every purpose under heaven.   5

A time to be born, a time to die,
A time to plant, a time to reap,
A time to kill, a time to heal,
A time to laugh, a time to weep.

To everything,   10
Turn, turn, turn,
There is a season,
Turn, turn, turn,
And a time to every purpose under heaven.

A time to build up, a time to break down,   15
A time to get, a time to want,
A time to cast away stones, a time to gather stones together.

To everything,
Turn, turn, turn,
There is a season,   20
Turn, turn, turn,
And a time to every purpose under heaven.

A time of love, a time of hate,
A time of war, a time of peace,
A time you may embrace, a time to refrain from embracing.   25

To everything,
Turn, turn, turn,
There is a season,
Turn, turn, turn,
And a time to every purpose under heaven.   30

A time to gain, a time to lose,
A time to rend, a time to sew,
A time for love, a time for hate,
A time for peace, I swear it's not too late.

This song is based on the following verses from Ecclesiastes (3:1–8):

To everything there is a season, and a time to every purpose under heaven:

A time to be born, and a time to die; a time to plant, and a time to pluck up that which is planted;

A time to kill, and a time to heal; a time to break down, and a time to build up;

A time to weep, and a time to laugh; a time to mourn, and a time to dance;

A time to cast away stones, and a time to gather stones together; a time to embrace, and a time to refrain from embracing;

A time to get, and a time to lose; a time to keep, and a time to cast away;

A time to rend, and a time to sew; a time to keep silence, and a time to speak;

A time to love, and a time to hate; a time of war, and a time of peace.

Sung by Pete Seeger, *Pete Seeger* (Columbia CS-8716). Also available on The Byrds, *Turn Turn Turn* (Columbia CS-9254); Judy Collins, *Recollections* (Elektra 74055); Nina Simone, *To Love Somebody* (Victor LSP-4152).

Richard Cory

Paul Simon (1942–   )

They say that Richard Cory owns one-half of this whole town,
With political connections to spread his wealth around.
Born into society, a banker's only child,
He had everything a man could want: power, grace and style.

But I work in his factory,   5
And I curse the life I'm living,
And I curse my poverty
And I wish that I could be
Richard Cory.

The papers print his picture almost everywhere he goes,   10
Richard Cory at the opera, Richard Cory at the show,
And the rumor of his parties, and the orgies on his yacht;
Oh, he surely must be happy with everything he's got.

But I work in his factory,
And I curse the life I'm living,   15
And I curse my poverty
And I wish that I could be
Richard Cory.

He freely gave to charity, he had the common touch,
And they were grateful for his patronage, and they thanked him very much. 20
So my mind is filled with wonder, when the evening headlines read:
"Richard Cory went home last night and put a bullet through his head."

But I work in his factory,
And I curse the life I'm living,
And I curse my poverty   25
And I wish that I could be
Richard Cory.

Based on Edwin Arlington Robinson's poem of the same title, which is printed on p. 34.

Sung by Simon and Garfunkel, *Sounds of Silence* (Columbia CS-9269).

"Richard Cory" © 1966 by Paul Simon. Used with the permission of the publisher.

And When I Die

Laura Nyro

I'm not scared of dyin
and I don't really care
if it's peace you find in dyin
well then let the time be near
if it's peace you find in dyin   5
when the dyin time is here
just bundle up my coffin
cause it's cold way down there
And when I die
and when I'm gone   10
there'll be one child born
and a world to carry on.

My troubles are many
they're as deep as a well
I swear there ain't no heaven   15
and I pray there ain't no hell
swear there ain't no heaven
and pray there ain't no hell
but I'll never know by livin
only my dyin will tell   20
And when I die
and when I'm gone
there'll be one child born
and a world to carry on.

Give me my freedom   25
for as long as I be
all I ask of livin
is to have no chains on me
all I ask of livin
and all I ask of dyin   30
is to go naturally.

Don't wanna go by the devil
don't wanna go by the demon
don't wanna go by Satan
don't wanna die uneasy   35
just let me go naturally

ιnd when I die
and when I'm gone
there'll be one child born
and a world to carry on.   40

Sung by Laura Nyro, *First Songs* (Verve-Forecast 3020). Also available on *Blood, Sweat and Tears* (Columbia CS-9720); Sammy Davis, Jr., *Something for Everybody* (Motown 710).

Long Time Gone

David Crosby (1941–   )

It's been a long time comin'
It's goin' to be a long time gone.
And it appears to be a long time,
Yes a long, long time before the dawn.

Turn, turn any corner,   5
Hear, you must hear what the people say.
You know there's something goin' on around here,
That surely, surely won't stand the light of day.

And it appears to be a long, appears to be a long
Time, such a long, long time before the dawn.   10

Speak out, you got to speak out against
The madness, you got to speak your mind, if you dare.
But don't try to get yourself elected,
If you do you had better cut your hair.

'Cause it appears to be a long,   15
Appears to be a long,
Appears to be a long
Time, before the dawn.

It's been a long time comin'
It's goin' to be a long time gone.   20

But you know,
The darkest hour is always just before the dawn.

And it appears to be a long,
Appears to be a long
Time, before the dawn.   25

Sung by Crosby, Stills and Nash, *Crosby, Stills and Nash* (Atlantic 8229).

Suite: Judy Blue Eyes

Stephen Stills

It's getting to the point
Where I'm no fun anymore,
I am sorry.
Sometimes it hurts so badly
I must cry out loud   5
I am lonely.
I am yours, you are mine,
You are what you are,
And you make it hard—

Remember what we've said, and done, and felt   10
About each other,
Oh babe, have mercy.
Don't let the past remind us of what we are not now.
I am not dreaming.
I am yours, you are mine,   15
You are what you are
And you make it hard.

Tearing yourself away from me now,
You are free and I am crying.
This does not mean I don't love you,   20
I do, that's forever, and always.
I am yours, you are mine,
You are what you are.
And you make it hard—

Something inside is telling me that   25
I've got your secret. Are you still listening:
Fear is the lock, and laughter is the key to your heart.
And I love you.
I am yours, you are mine,
And you are what you are.   30
And you make it hard, and you make it hard.

Friday evening, Sunday in the afternoon,
What have you got to lose?
Tuesday morning, please be gone, I'm tired of you.
What have you got to lose?   35
Can I tell it like it is? Help me, I'm suffering.
Listen to me baby. Help me, I'm dying.
That's what I've got to lose.
I've got an answer,
I'm going to fly away, what have I got to lose?   40
Will you come to see me Thursdays and Saturdays?
What have you got to lose?

Chestnut brown canary, ruby throated sparrow.
Sing a song, don't be long,
Thrill me to the marrow.   45

Voices of the angels, ring around the moonlight,
Asking me, said she's so free,
How can you catch the sparrow?

Lacy lilting lady, losing love lamenting,
Change my life, make it right,   50
Be my lady.

For What It's Worth

Stephen Stills

There's something happenin' here.
What it is ain't exactly clear.
There's a man with a gun over there,
Tellin' me I've got to beware.
It's time we stop, children,   5
What's that sound?
Everybody look what's goin' down.

There's battle lines bein' drawn,
Nobody's right if everybody's wrong.
Young people speakin' their minds,   10
Gettin' so much resistance from behind.
It's time we stop, children,
What's that sound?
Everybody look what's goin' down.

What a field day for the heat.   15
A thousand people in the street,
Singin' songs and carryin' signs.
Mostly saying, "Hooray for our side."
It's time we stop, children,
What's that sound?   20
Everybody look what's goin' down.

Paranoia strikes deep,
Into your life it will creep.
It starts when you're always afraid,
Step out of line, the Man come   25
And take you away.
You better stop, hey,
What's that sound?
Everybody look what's goin' down.

Sung by Buffalo Springfield, *Buffalo Springfield* (Atco 200). Also available on Miriam
Makeba, *Keep Me in Mind* (Reprise 6381); Cher, *Cher* (Atco 298); *Voices of East Harlem*
(Elektra 74080).

Society's Child

Janis Ian (1951–   )

Come to my door, baby.
Face is clean and shining black as night.
My mother went to answer.
You know that you looked so fine.
Now I could understand your tears and your shame,   5
She called you boy instead of your name.
When she wouldn't let you inside,
When she turned and said, "But, honey, he's not our kind."
She says I can't see you anymore,
Baby, can't see you anymore.   10

199

Walk me down to school, baby,
Everybody's acting deaf and blind,
Until they turn and say,
"Why don't you stick to your own kind?"
My teachers all laugh their smirking stares,   15
Cutting deep down in our affairs.
Preachers of equality, think they believe it,
Then why won't they just let us be?
They say I can't see you anymore,
Baby, can't see you anymore.   20

One of these days I'm gonna stop my listening,
Gonna raise my head up high,
One of these days I'm gonna raise up my glistening wings and fly.
But that day will have to wait for a while.
Baby, I'm only society's child.   25
When we're older things may change,
But for now this is the way they must remain.
I say I can't see you anymore,
Baby, I can't see you anymore.
No, I don't want to see you anymore, baby.   30

Sung by Janis Ian, *Janis Ian* (MGM 121). Also available on Janis Ian, *Core of the Rock* (MGM 4669).

Goodbye and Hello

Tim Buckley (1947–   )

The antique people are down in the dungeons
Run by machines and afraid of the tax
Their heads in the grave and their hands on their eyes.
Hauling their hearts around circular tracks
Pretending forever their masquerade towers   5
Are not really riddled with widening cracks
And I wave goodbye to iron
And smile hello to the air.

O the new children dance   I am young
All around the balloons.   I will live   10
Swaying by chance   I am strong
To the breeze from the moon.   I can give
Painting the sky   You the strange
With the colors of sun.   Seed of day
Freely they fly   Feel the change   15
As all become one.   Know the way.

The velocity addicts explode on the highways
Ignoring the journey and moving so fast
Their nerves fall apart and they gasp, but can't breathe.
They run from the cops of the skeleton past   20
Petrified by tradition in a nightmare they stagger
Into nowhere at all and then look up aghast
And I wave goodbye to speed
And smile hello to a rose.

O the new children play   I am young   25
Under juniper trees.   I will live
Sky blue or grey,   I am strong
They continue at ease.   I can give
Moving so slow   You the strange
That serenely they can   Seed of day   30
Gracefully grow,   Feel the change
And yes, still understand.   Know the way.

The king and the queen in their castle of billboards
Sleepwalk down the hallways dragging behind
All their possessions and transient treasures   35
As they go to worship the electronic shrine
On which is playing the late late commercial
In that hollowest house of the opulent blind
And I wave goodbye to Mammon
And smile hello to a stream.   40

O the new children buy   I am young
All the world for a song,   I will live
Without a dime   I am strong
To which they belong.   I can give
Nobody owns   You the strange   45
Anything anywhere,   Seed of day
Everyone's grown   Feel the change
Yes so big they can share.   Know the way.

The vaudeville generals cavort on the stage
And shatter their audience with submachine guns   50
And Freedom and Violence the acrobat clowns,
Do a balancing act on the graves of our sons
While the tapdancing emperor sings "War is Peace,"
And Love the Magician disappears in the fun,
And I wave goodbye to murder   55
And smile hello to the rain.

O the new children can't	I am young
Tell a foe from a friend	I will live
Quick to enchant	I am strong
And so glad to extend	I can give 60
Handfuls of dawn	You the strange
To kaleidoscope men	Seed of day
Come from beyond	Feel the change
The great wall of skin.	Know the way.

The bloodless husbands are jesters who listen   65
Like sheep to the shrieks and commands of their wives,
And the men who aren't men leave the women alone
See them all faking love on a bed made of knives,
Afraid to discover or trust in their bodies
And in secret divorce they will never survive,   70
And I wave goodbye to ashes
And smile hello to a girl.

O the new children kiss,	I am young
They are so proud to learn	I will live
Womanhood bliss,	I am strong 75
And the manfire that burns	I can give
Knowing no fear	You the strange
They take off their clothes	Seed of day
Honest and clear	Feel the change
As a river that flows.	Know the way. 80

The antique people are fading out slowly,
Like newspapers flaming in mind suicide,
Godless and sexless directionless looms
Their sham sandcastles dissolve in the tide
They put on their deathmasks and compromise daily   85
The new children will live for the elders have died
And I wave goodbye to America
And I smile hello to the world.

Sung by Tim Buckley, *Goodbye and Hello* (Elektra EKS-7318).

202

My Country 'Tis of Thy People You're Dying

Buffy Sainte-Marie (1941–   )

Now that your big eyes have finally opened
Now that you're wondering how must they feel
Meaning them that you've chased across America's movie screens
Now that you're wondering how can it be real
That the ones you call colorful, noble and proud   5
In your school propaganda
They starve in their splendor
You've asked for my comment, I simply will render

My country 'tis of thy people you're dying.

Now that the long houses breed superstition   10
You force us to send our toddlers away
To your schools where they're taught to despise their traditions
Forbid them their languages, then further say
That American history really began
When Columbus set sail out of Europe and stress   15
That the nation of leeches that conquered this land
Are the biggest and bravest, and boldest and best
And yet where in your history books is the tale
Of the genocide basic to this country's birth
Of the preachers that lied, how the Bill of Rights failed   20
How a nation of patriots returned to the earth
And where will it tell of the Liberty Bell
As it rang with a thud o'er the tinsel of mud
And of brave Uncle Sam in Alaska this year

My country 'tis of thy people you're dying.   25

Hear how the bargain was made for the West
With her shivering children in zero degrees
Blankets for your land so the treaties attest
Oh well, blankets for land is a bargain indeed
And the blankets were those Uncle Sam had collected   30
From smallpox disease dying soldiers that day
And the tribes were wiped out and the history books censored
A hundred years of your statesmen have felt it better this way
Yet a few of the conquered have somehow survived

Their blood runs redder though genes have been paled   35
From the Grand Canyon's caverns to the Craven Red Hills
The wounded, the losers, the rod sings their tale
From Los Angeles county to upstate New York
The white nation fattens while others grow lean
Oh, the tricked and evicted, they know what I mean   40

My country 'tis of thy people you're dying.

The past it just crumbled, the future just threatens
Our lifeblood shut up in your chemical tanks
And now here you come, bill of sale in your hand
And surprise in eyes that we're lacking in thanks   45
For the blessings of civilization you brought us
The lessons you've taught us, the ruin you've wrought us
Oh, see what our trust in America's brought us

My country 'tis of thy people you're dying.

Now that the pride of the sires receive charity   50
Now that we're harmless and safe behind laws
Now that my life's to be known as your heritage
Now that even the graves have been robbed
Now that our own chosen way is a novelty
Hands on our hearts, we salute you your victory   55
Choke on your blue, white and scarlet hypocrisy
Pitying the blindness that you've never seen
That the eagles of war whose wings lent you glory
They were never no more than carrion crows
Push the wrens from their nest, stow their eggs, change their story   60
The mockingbird sings it, it's all that she knows
Oh, what can I do, say a powerless few
With a lump in your throat and a tear in your eye,
Can't you see that our poverty's profiting you?

My country 'tis of thy people you're dying.   65

Sung by Buffy Sainte-Marie, *Little Wheel Spin and Spin* (Vanguard 79211).

Draft Dodger Rag

Phil Ochs (1940–   )

I'm just a typical American boy
From a typical American town,
I believe in God and Senator Dodd,
And in keeping old Castro down.

And when it came my time to serve,   5
I knew better dead than red,
But when I got to my old draft board,
Buddy, this is what I said:

Sarge, I'm only eighteen.
I've got a ruptured spleen   10
And I always carry a purse.
I've got eyes like a bat
And my feet are flat.
My asthma is getting worse.

Consider my career,   15
My sweetheart dear,
And my poor old invalid aunt.
Besides I ain't no fool,
I am a-going to school
And I'm working in a defense plant.   20

I got a dislocated disc,
And a wrapped-up back
And I'm allergic to flowers and bugs.
And when a bomb shell hits
I get epileptic fits,   25
And I'm addicted to a thousand drugs.

I've got the weakness woes
And I can't touch my toes.
I can hardly reach my knees.
And if the enemy ever came close to me   30
I'd probably start to sneeze.

Sarge, I'm only eighteen.
I've got a ruptured spleen,
And always carry a purse.
I've got eyes like a bat   35
And my feet are flat.
My asthma is getting worse.

Consider my career,
My sweetheart dear,
And my poor invalid aunt.   40
Besides I ain't no fool,
I am a-going to school
And I'm working in a defense plant.

I hate Chou En-Lai
And I hope he dies   45
But I think you gotta see
That if someone got to go over there
That someone isn't me

So have a ball,
Sarge, watch 'em fall,   50
While you kill me a thousand or so.
And if you ever get a war without any gore
Well, I'll be the first to go.

Sarge, I'm only eighteen.
I've got a ruptured spleen,   55
And I always carry a purse.
I've got eyes like a bat
And my feet are flat.
My asthma's getting worse.

Consider my career,   60
My sweetheart dear,
I got to water my rubber-tree plant.
Besides I ain't no fool,
I am a-going to school,
And I'm working in a defense plant.   65

Sarge, I'm only eighteen.
I've got a ruptured spleen,
And I always carry a purse.
I've got eyes like a bat
And my feet are flat.   70
My asthma's getting worse.

Consider my career,
My sweetheart dear,
My poor old invalid aunt.
Besides I ain't no fool,   75
I am a-going to school
And I'm working in a defense plant.

Sung by Phil Ochs, *I Ain't Marching Anymore* (Elektra EKS-7827).

Pollution

Tom Lehrer (1928–   )

If you visit American city,
You will find it very pretty.
Just two things of which you must beware:
Don't drink the water and don't breathe the air.
Pollution, pollution,   5
They got smog and sewage and mud,
Turn on your tap and get hot and cold running crud.

See the halibuts and the sturgeons
Being wiped out by detergents.

Fish got to swim and birds got to fly   10
But they don't last long if they try.

Pollution, pollution,
You can use the latest toothpaste,
And then rinse your mouth with industrial waste.

Just go out for a breath of air,   15
And you'll be ready for Medicare.
The city streets are really quite a thrill,
If the hoods don't get you, the monoxide will.

Pollution, pollution,
Wear a gas mask and a veil.   20
Then you can breathe, long as you don't inhale.

Lots of things there that you can drink,
But stay away from the kitchen sink.
Throw out your breakfast garbage, and I've got a hunch
That the folks downstream will drink it for lunch.   25

So go to the city, see the crazy people there.
Like lambs to the slaughter
They're drinking the water
And breathing the air.

Sung by Tom Lehrer, *That Was the Year That Was* (Reprise 6179).

my father moved through dooms of love

e. e. cummings (1894–1962)

my father moved through dooms of love
through sames of am through haves of give,
singing each morning out of each night
my father moved through depths of height

this motionless forgetful where   5
turn at his glance to shining here;
that if(so timid air is firm)
under his eyes would stir and squirm

newly as from unburied which
floats the first who,his april touch   10
drove sleeping selves to swarm their fates
woke dreamers to their ghostly roots

and should some why completely weep
my father's fingers brought her sleep:
vainly no smallest voice might cry   15
for he could feel the mountains grow.

Lifting the valleys of the sea
my father moved through griefs of joy;
praising a forehead called the moon
singing desire into begin   20

joy was his song and joy so pure
a heart of star by him could steer
and pure so now and now so yes
the wrists of twilight would rejoice

keen as midsummer's keen beyond   25
conceiving mind of sun will stand,
so strictly(over utmost him
so hugely)stood my father's dream

his flesh was flesh his blood was blood:
no hungry man but wished him food;   30
no cripple wouldn't creep one mile
uphill to only see him smile.

Scorning the pomp of must and shall
my father moved through dooms of feel;
his anger was as right as rain   35
his pity was as green as grain

septembering arms of year extend
less humbly wealth to foe and friend
than he to foolish and to wise
offered immeasurable is   40

proudly and(by octobering flame
beckoned)as earth will downward climb,
so naked for immortal work
his shoulders marched against the dark

his sorrow was as true as bread: 45
no liar looked him in the head;
if every friend became his foe
he'd laugh and build a world with snow.

My father moved through theys of we,
singing each new leaf out of each tree   50
(and every child was sure that spring
danced when she heard my father sing)

then let men kill which cannot share,
let blood and flesh be mud and mire,
scheming imagine,passion willed,   55
freedom a drug that's bought and sold

giving to steal and cruel kind,
a heart to fear,to doubt a mind,

209

to differ a disease of same,
conform the pinnacle of am   60

though dull were all we taste as bright,
bitter all utterly things sweet,
maggoty minus and dumb death
all we inherit,all bequeath

and nothing quite so least as truth   65
—i say though hate were why men breathe—
because my father lived his soul
love is the whole and more than all

Read by the author on *Twentieth Century Poetry in English* (Library of Congress P-L5).

Elegy for Jane

Theodore Roethke (1908–1963)

(My Student, Thrown by a Horse)

I remember the neckcurls, limp and damp as tendrils;
And her quick look, a sidelong pickerel smile;
And how, once startled into talk, the light syllables leaped for her,
And she balanced in the delight of her thought,
A wren, happy, tail into the wind,   5
Her song trembling the twigs and small branches.
The shade sang with her;
The leaves, their whispers turned to kissing;
And the mould sang in the bleached valleys under the rose.

Oh, when she was sad, she cast herself down into such a pure depth,   10
Even a father could not find her:
Scraping her cheek against straw;
Stirring the clearest water.

My sparrow, you are not here,
Waiting like a fern, making a spiney shadow.   15
The sides of wet stones cannot console me,
Nor the moss, wound with the last light.

If only I could nudge you from this sleep,
My maimed darling, my skittery pigeon.
Over this damp grave I speak the words of my love: 20
I, with no rights in this matter,
Neither father nor lover.

Read by the author on *An Album of Modern Poetry* (Library of Congress 2019).

The Love Song of J. Alfred Prufrock

T. S. Eliot (1888–1965)

S'io credesse che mia risposta fosse
A persona che mai tornasse al mondo,
Questa fiamma staria senza piu scosse.
Ma perciocche giammai di questo fondo
Non torno vivo alcun, s'i'odo il vero,
Senza tema d'infamia ti rispondo.

Let us go then, you and I,
When the evening is spread out against the sky
Like a patient etherized upon a table;
Let us go, through certain half-deserted streets,
The muttering retreats   5
Of restless nights in one-night cheap hotels
And sawdust restaurants with oyster-shells:
Streets that follow like a tedious argument
Of insidious intent
To lead you to an overwhelming question. . .   10
Oh, do not ask, 'What is it?'
Let us go and make our visit.

In the room the women come and go
Talking of Michelangelo.

The yellow fog that rubs its back upon the window-panes,   15
The yellow smoke that rubs its muzzle on the window-panes
Licked its tongue into the corners of the evening,
Lingered upon the pools that stand in drains,
Let fall upon its back the soot that falls from chimneys,
Slipped by the terrace, made a sudden leap,   20
And seeing that it was a soft October night,
Curled once about the house, and fell asleep.

And indeed there will be time
For the yellow smoke that slides along the street,
Rubbing its back upon the window-panes;   25
There will be time, there will be time
To prepare a face to meet the faces that you meet;
There will be time to murder and create,
And time for all the works and days of hands
That lift and drop a question on your plate;   30
Time for you and time for me,
And time yet for a hundred indecisions,
And for a hundred visions and revisions,
Before the taking of a toast and tea.

In the room the women come and go   35
Talking of Michelangelo.

And indeed there will be time
To wonder, 'Do I dare?' and, 'Do I dare?'
Time to turn back and descend the stair,
With a bald spot in the middle of my hair—   40
(They will say: 'How his hair is growing thin!')
My morning coat, my collar mounting firmly to the chin,
My necktie rich and modest, but asserted by a simple pin—
(They will say: 'But how his arms and legs are thin!')
Do I dare   45
Disturb the universe?
In a minute there is time
For decisions and revisions which a minute will reverse.

For I have known them all already, known them all:—
Have known the evenings, mornings, afternoons,   50
I have measured out my life with coffee spoons;
I know the voices dying with a dying fall
Beneath the music from a farther room.
   So how should I presume?

And I have known the eyes already, known them all—   55
The eyes that fix you in a formulated phrase,
And when I am formulated, sprawling on a pin,
When I am pinned and wriggling on the wall,
Then how should I begin
To spit out all the butt-ends of my days and ways?   60
   And how should I presume?

And I have known the arms already, known them all—
Arms that are braceleted and white and bare
(But in the lamplight, downed with light brown hair!)

212

Is it perfume from a dress   65
That makes me so digress?
Arms that lie along a table, or wrap about a shawl.
    And should I then presume?
    And how should I begin?

                        .   .   .   .   .

Shall I say, I have gone at dusk through narrow streets   70
And watched the smoke that rises from the pipes
Of lonely men in shirt-sleeves, leaning out of windows? . . .

I should have been a pair of ragged claws
Scuttling across the floors of silent seas.

                        .   .   .   .   .

And the afternoon, the evening, sleeps so peacefully!   75
Smoothed by long fingers,
Asleep . . . tired . . . or it malingers,
Stretched on the floor, here beside you and me.
Should I, after tea and cakes and ices,
Have the strength to force the moment to its crisis?   80
But though I have wept and fasted, wept and prayed,
Though I have seen my head (grown slightly bald) brought in
        upon a platter,
I am no prophet—and here's no great matter;
I have seen the moment of my greatness flicker,
And I have seen the eternal Footman hold my coat, and snicker, 85
And in short, I was afraid.

And would it have been worth it, after all,
After the cups, the marmalade, the tea,
Among the porcelain, among some talk of you and me,
Would it have been worth while,   90
To have bitten off the matter with a smile,
To have squeezed the universe into a ball
To roll it toward some overwhelming question,
To say: 'I am Lazarus, come from the dead,
Come back to tell you all, I shall tell you all'—   95
If one, settling a pillow by her head,
    Should say: 'That is not what I meant at all,
    That is not it, at all.'

                        .   .   .   .   .

And would it have been worth it, after all,
Would it have been worth while,   100
After the sunsets and the dooryards and the sprinkled streets,

213

After the novels, after the teacups, after the skirts that trail along
    the floor —
And this, and so much more? —
It is impossible to say just what I mean!
But as if a magic lantern threw the nerves in patterns on a screen: 105
Would it have been worth while
If one, settling a pillow or throwing off a shawl,
And turning toward the window, should say:
    'That is not it at all,
    That is not what I meant, at all.'   110

No! I am not Prince Hamlet, nor was meant to be;
Am an attendant lord, one that will do
To swell a progress, start a scene or two,
Advise the prince; no doubt, an easy tool,
Deferential, glad to be of use,   115
Politic, cautious, and meticulous;
Full of high sentence, but a bit obtuse;
At times, indeed, almost ridiculous —
Almost, at times, the Fool.

I grow old . . . I grow old . . .   120
I shall wear the bottoms of my trousers rolled.

Shall I part my hair behind? Do I dare to eat a peach?
I shall wear white flannel trousers, and walk upon the beach.
I have heard the mermaids singing, each to each.

I do not think that they will sing to me.   125

I have seen them riding seaward on the waves
Combing the white hair of the waves blown back
When the wind blows the water white and black.

We have lingered in the chambers of the sea
By sea-girls wreathed with seaweed red and brown   130
Till human voices wake us, and we drown.

epigraph: In Dante's *Inferno,* a man condemned to hell confesses the evil of his life to a
visitor. In this passage, he says that he would not have made the confession if he thought
his story would reach the ears of the living.

Read by the author on *T. S. Eliot Reading Poems and Choruses* (Caedmon TC-1045).

Junkman's Obbligato

Lawrence Ferlinghetti (1919–   )

Let's go
Come on
Let's go
Empty out our pockets
and disappear   5
Missing all our appointments
and turning up unshaven
years later
old cigarette papers
stuck to our pants   10
leaves in our hair.
Let us not
worry about the payments
anymore.
Let them come   15
and take it away
whatever it was
we were paying for.
And us with it.

Let us arise and go now   20
to where dogs do it
Over the Hill
where they keep the earthquakes
behind the city dumps
lost among gasmains and garbage.   25
Let us see the City Dumps
for what they are.
My country tears of thee.
Let us disappear
in automobile graveyards   30
and reappear years later
picking rags and newspapers
drying our drawers
on garbage fires
patches on our ass.   35
Do not bother
to say goodbye
to anyone.
Your missus will not miss us.

Let's go   40
smelling of sterno
where the benches are filled
with discarded Bowling Green statues
in the interior dark night
of the flowery bowery   45
our eyes watery
with the contemplation
of empty bottles of muscatel.
Let us recite from broken bibles
on streetcorners   50
Follow dogs on docks
Speak wild songs
Throw stones
Say anything
Blink at the sun and scratch   55
and stumble into silence
Diddle in doorways
Know whores thirdhand
after everyone else is finished
Stagger befuddled into East River sunsets   60
Sleep in phone booths
Puke in pawnshops
wailing for a winter overcoat.

Let us arise and go now
under the city   65
where ashcans roll
and reappear in putrid clothes
as the uncrowned underground kings
of subway men's rooms.
Let us feed the pigeons   70
at the City Hall
urging them to do their duty
in the Mayor's office.
Hurry up please it's time.
The end is coming.   75
Flash floods
Disasters in the sun
Dogs unleashed
Sister in the street
her brassiere backwards.   80

Let us arise and go now
into the interior dark night
of the soul's still bowery
and find ourselves anew

where subways stall and wait   85
under the River
Cross over
into full puzzlement.
South Ferry will not run forever
They are cutting out the Bay ferries   90
but it is still not too late
to get lost in Oakland.
Washington has not yet toppled
from his horse.
There is still time to goose him   95
and go
leaving our income tax form behind
and our waterproof wristwatch with it
staggering blind after alleycats
under Brooklyn's Bridge   100
blown statues in baggy pants
our tincan cries and garbage voices
trailing.
Junk for sale!

Let's cut out let's go   105
into the real interior of the country
where hockshops reign
mere unblind anarchy upon us.
The end is here
but golf goes on at Burning Tree.   110
It's raining it's pouring
The Ole Man is snoring.
Another flood is coming
though not the kind you think.
There is still time to sink   115
and think.
I wish to descend in society.
I wish to make like free.
Swing low sweet chariot.
Let us not wait for the cadillacs   120
to carry us triumphant
into the interior
waving at the natives
like roman senators in the provinces
wearing poet's laurels   125
on lighted brows.
Let us not wait for the write-up
on page one
of The New York Times Book Review

217

images of insane success 130
smiling from the photo.
By the time they print your picture
in Life Magazine
you will have become a negative anyway
a print with a glossy finish. 135
They will have come and gotten you
to be famous
and you still will not be free.
Goodbye I'm going.
I'm selling everything 140
and giving away the rest
to the Good Will Industries.
It will be dark out there
with the Salvation Army Band.
And the mind its own illumination. 145
Goodbye I'm walking out on the whole scene.
Close down the joint.
The system is all loused up.
Rome was never like this.
I'm tired of waiting for Godot. 150
I am going where turtles win
I am going
where conmen puke and die
Down the sad esplanades
of the official world. 155
Junk for sale!
My country tears of thee.

Let us go then you and I
leaving our neckties behind on lampposts
Take up the full beard 160
of walking anarchy
looking like Walt Whitman
a homemade bomb in the pocket.
I wish to descend in the social scale.
High society is low society. 165
I am a social climber
climbing downward
And the descent is difficult.
The Upper Middle Class Ideal
is for the birds 170
but the birds have no use for it
having their own kind of pecking order
based upon birdsong.
Pigeons on the grass alas.

218

Let us arise and go now
to the Isle of Manisfree.
Let loose the hogs of peace.
Hurry up please it's time.
Let us arise and go now
into the interior   180
of Foster's Cafeteria.
So long Emily Post.
So long
Lowell Thomas.
Goodbye Broadway.   185
Goodbye Herald Square.
Turn it off.
Confound the system.
Cancel all our leases.
Lose the War   190
without killing anybody.
Let horses scream
and ladies run
to flushless powderrooms.
The end has just begun.   195
I want to announce it.
Run don't walk
to the nearest exit.
The real earthquake is coming.
I can feel the building shake.   200
I am the refined type.
I cannot stand it.
I am going
where asses lie down
with customs collectors who call themselves   205
literary critics.
My tool is dusty.
My body hung up too long
in strange suspenders.
Get me a bright bandana   210
for a jockstrap.
Turn loose and we'll be off
where sports cars collapse
and the world begins again.
Hurry up please it's time.   215
It's time and a half
and there's the rub.
The thinkpad makes homeboys of us all.
Let us cut out
into stray eternity.   220

219

ds are full of larks.
d is swinging.
hee

now   225
to the Isle of Manisfree
and live the true blue simple life
of wisdom and wonderment
where all things grow
straight up   230
aslant and singing
in the yellow sun
poppies out of cowpods
thinking angels out of turds.
I must arise and go now   235
to the Isle of Manisfree
way up behind the broken words
and woods of Arcady.

Read by author, with jazz background, on *Poetry Readings in the Cellar* (Fantasy 7002).

from **The People, Yes**

Carl Sandburg (1878–1967)

   The people, yes, the people,
Until the people are taken care of one way or another,
Until the people are solved somehow for the day and·hour,
Until then one hears "Yes but the people what about the people?"
Sometimes as though the people is a child to be pleased or fed   5
Or again a hoodlum you have to be tough with
And seldom as though the people is a caldron and a reservoir
Of the human reserves that shape history.

. . .

   Fire, chaos, shadows,
Events trickling from a thin line of flame   10
On into cries and combustions never expected:
The people have the element of surprise.

. . .

"The czar has eight million men with guns and bayonets.
"Nothing can happen to the czar.
"The czar is the voice of God and shall live forever.   15
"Turn and look at the forest of steel and cannon
"Where the czar is guarded by eight million soldiers.
"Nothing can happen to the czar."

They said that for years and in the summer of 1914

.   .   .

As a portent and an assurance they said with owl faces: 20
   "Nothing can happen to the czar."
Yet the czar and his bodyguard of eight million vanished
And the czar stood in a cellar before a little firing squad
And the command of fire was given
And the czar stepped into regions of mist and ice   25
The czar travelled into an ethereal uncharted siberia
While two kaisers also vanished from thrones
Ancient and established in blood and iron —
Two kaisers backed by ten million bayonets
Had their crowns in a gutter, their palaces mobbed.   30
      In fire, chaos, shadows,
In hurricanes beyond foretelling of probabilities,
In the shove and whirl of unforeseen combustions
The people, yes, the people,
Move eternally in the elements of surprise,   35
Changing from hammer to bayonet and back to hammer,
The hallelujah chorus forever shifting its star soloists.

The people learn, unlearn, learn,
a builder, a wrecker, a builder again,
a juggler of shifting puppets.   40
   In so few eyeblinks
   In transition lightning streaks,
the people project midgets into giants,
the people shrink titans into dwarfs.

   Faiths blow on the winds   45
   and become shibboleths
   and deep growths
   with men ready to die
for a living word on the tongue,
for a light alive in the bones,   50
for dreams fluttering in the wrists.

.   .   .

221

Sleep is a suspension midway
and a conundrum of shadows
lost in meadows of the moon.
   The people sleep. 55
   Ai! ai! the people sleep.
Yet the sleepers toss in sleep
and an end comes of sleep
and the sleepers wake.
   Ai! ai! the sleepers wake! 60

. . .

The storm of propaganda blows always.
In every air of today the germs float and hover.
   The people have the say-so.
   Let the argument go on.
   Let the people listen. 65
Tomorrow the people say Yes or No by one question:
   "What else can be done?"
In the drive of faiths on the wind today the people know:
"We have come far and we are going farther yet."

. . .

   The people will live on. 70
The learning and blundering people will live on.
   They will be tricked and sold and again sold
And go back to the nourishing earth for rootholds,
   The people so peculiar in renewal and comeback,
   You can't laugh off their capacity to take it. 75
The mammoth rests between his cyclonic dramas.

. . .

The people is a tragic and comic two-face:
hero and hoodlum: phantom and gorilla twist-
ing to moan with a gargoyle mouth: "They
buy me and sell me . . . it's a game . . . 80
sometime I'll break loose . . ."

. . .

   Now the steel mill sky is alive.
   The fire breaks white and zigzag
   shot on a gun-metal gloaming.
   Man is a long time coming. 85
   Man will yet win.
   Brother may yet line up with brother:

This old anvil laughs at many broken hammers.
   There are men who can't be bought.
   The fireborn are at home in fire.   90
   The stars make no noise.
   You can't hinder the wind from blowing.
   Time is a great teacher.
   Who can live without hope?

In the darkness with a great bundle of grief   95
   the people march.
In the night, and overhead a shovel of stars for
   keeps, the people march:
               "Where to? what next?"
               "Where to? what next?"   100

Read by the author on *Carl Sandburg Reads the Poems of Carl Sandburg* (Decca DL-9039).

Good Morning

Langston Hughes (1902–1967)

Good morning, daddy!
I was born here, he said,
watched Harlem grow
until colored folks spread
from river to river   5
across the middle of Manhattan
out of Penn Station
dark tenth of a nation,
planes from Puerto Rico,
and holds of boats, chico,   10
up from Cuba Haiti Jamaica,
in busses marked New York
from Georgia Florida Louisiana Arkansas
to Harlem Brooklyn the Bronx
but most of all to Harlem   15
dusky sash across Manhattan

"Good Morning" from *Montage of a Dream Deferred*. Reprinted by permission of Harold Ober Associates Incorporated. Copyright 1951 by Langston Hughes.

I've seen them come dark
   wondering
   wide-eyed
   dreaming   20
out of Penn Station —
but the trains are late.
The gates open —
yet there're bars
at each gate.   25

Read by the author on *Weary Blues* (Verve VSP-36).

Dream Deferred

Langston Hughes (1902–1967)

What happens to a dream deferred?
Does it dry up
like a raisin in the sun?
Or fester like a sore —
And then run?   5
Does it stink like rotten meat?
Or crust and sugar over —
like a syrupy sweet?

Maybe it just sags
like a heavy load.   10

Or does it explode?

Read by the author on *Weary Blues* (Verve VSP-36).

Same in Blues

Langston Hughes (1902–1967)

I said to my baby,
Baby, take it slow.
I can't, she said, I can't!
I got to go!

    There's a certain   5
    amount of traveling
    in a dream deferred.

Lulu said to Leonard,
I want a diamond ring.
Leonard said to Lulu,   10
You won't get a goddamn thing!

    A certain
    amount of nothing
    in a dream deferred.

Daddy, daddy, daddy,   15
All I want is you.
You can have me, baby —
but my lovin' days is through.

    A certain
    amount of impotence   20
    in a dream deferred.

Three parties
On my party line —
But that third party,
Lord, ain't mine!   25

    There's liable
    to be confusion
    in a dream deferred.

From river to river
Uptown and down,   30
There's liable to be confusion
when a dream gets kicked around.

You talk like
they don't kick
dreams around   35
Downtown.

I expect they do —
But I'm talking about
Harlem to you!
Harlem to you!   40
Harlem to you!
Harlem to you!

Freedom

Langston Hughes (1902–1967)

Freedom will not come
Today, this year
    Nor ever
Through compromise and fear.

I have as much right   5
As the other fellow has
    To stand
On my two feet
And own the land.

I tire so of hearing people say,   10
Let things take their course.
Tomorrow is another day.
I do not need my freedom when I'm dead.
I cannot live on tomorrow's bread.
    Freedom   15
    Is a strong seed
    Planted
    In a great need.
    I live here, too.
    I want freedom   20
    Just as you.

The Return

Arna Bontemps (1902–   )

I

Once more, listening to the wind and rain,
Once more, you and I, and above the hurting sound
Of these comes back the throbbing of remembered rain,
Treasured rain falling on dark ground.
Once more, huddling birds upon the leaves   5
And summer trembling on a withered vine.
And once more, returning out of pain,
The friendly ghost that was your love and mine.

II

Darkness brings the jungle to our room:
The throb of rain is the throb of muffled drums.   10
Darkness hangs our room with pendulums
Of vine and in the gathering gloom
Our walls recede into a denseness of
Surrounding trees. This is a night of love
Retained from those lost nights our fathers slept   15
In huts; this is a night that must not die.
Let us keep the dance of rain our fathers kept
And tread our dreams beneath the jungle sky.

III

And now the downpour ceases.
Let us go back once more upon the glimmering leaves   20
And as the throbbing of the drums increases
Shake the grass and dripping boughs of trees.
A dry wind stirs the palm; the old tree grieves.

Time has charged the years: the old days have returned.

Let us dance by metal waters burned   25
With gold of moon, let us dance
With naked feet beneath the young spice trees.
What was that light, that radiance
On your face? — something I saw when first
You passed beneath the jungle tapestries?   30

227

A moment we pause to quench our thirst
Kneeling at the water's edge, the gleam
Upon your face is plain: you have wanted this.
Let us go back and search the tangled dream
And as the muffled drum-beats throb and miss   35
Remember again how early darkness comes
To dreams and silence to the drums.

                        IV

Let us go back into the dusk again,
Slow and sad-like following the track
Of blowing leaves and cool white rain   40
Into the old gray dream, let us go back.
Our walls close about us we lie and listen
To the noise of the street, the storm and the driven birds.
A question shapes your lips, your eyes glisten
Retaining tears, but there are no more words.   45

Read by the author on *Anthology of Negro Poets in the USA* (Folkways FL-9791).

Heritage

Countee Cullen (1903–1946)

for Harold Jackman

What is Africa to me:
Copper sun or scarlet sea,
Jungle star or jungle track,
Strong bronzed men, or regal black
Women from whose loins I sprang   5
When the birds of Eden sang?
One three centuries removed
From the scenes his fathers loved,
Spicy grove, cinnamon tree,
What is Africa to me?   10

So I lie, who all day long
Want no sound except the song
Sung by wild barbaric birds
Goading massive jungle herds,

228

Juggernauts of flesh that pass   15
Trampling tall defiant grass
Where young forest lovers lie,
Plighting troth beneath the sky.
So I lie, who always hear,
Though I cram against my ear   20
Both my thumbs, and keep them there,
Great drums throbbing through the air.
So I lie, whose fount of pride,
Dear distress, and joy allied,
Is my somber flesh and skin,   25
With the dark blood dammed within
Like great pulsing tides of wine
That, I fear, must burst the fine
Channels of the chafing net
Where they surge and foam and fret.   30

Africa? A book one thumbs
Listlessly, till slumber comes.
Unremembered are her bats
Circling through the night, her cats
Crouching in the river reeds,   35
Stalking gentle flesh that feeds
By the river brink; no more
Does the bugle-throated roar
Cry that monarch claws have leapt
From the scabbards where they slept.   40
Silver snakes that once a year
Doff the lovely coats you wear,
See no covert in your fear
Lest a mortal eye should see;
What's your nakedness to me?   45
Here no leprous flowers rear
Fierce corollas in the air;
Here no bodies sleek and wet,
Dripping mingled rain and sweat,
Tread the savage measures of   50
Jungle boys and girls in love.
What is last year's snow to me,
Last year's anything? The tree
Budding yearly must forget
How its past arose or set—   55
Bough and blossom, flower, fruit,
Even what shy bird with mute
Wonder at her travail there,
Meekly labored in its hair.
One three centuries removed,   60
From the scenes his fathers loved,

229

Spicy grove, cinnamon tree,
What is Africa to me?

So I lie, who find no peace
Night or day, no slight release   65
From the unremittent beat
Made by cruel padded feet
Walking through my body's street.
Up and down they go, and back,
Treading out a jungle track.   70
So I lie, who never quite
Safely sleep from rain at night—
I can never rest at all
When the rain begins to fall;
Like a soul gone bad with pain   75
I must match its weird refrain;
Ever must I twist and squirm,
Writhing like a baited worm,
While its primal measures drip
Through my body, crying, "Strip!   80
Doff this new exuberance.
Come and dance the Lover's Dance!"
In an old remembered way
Rain works on me night and day.

Quaint, outlandish heathen gods   85
Black men fashion out of rods,
Clay, and brittle bits of stone,
In a likeness like their own,
My conversion came high-priced;
I belong to Jesus Christ,   90
Preacher of humility;
Heathen gods are naught to me.
Father, Son, and Holy Ghost,
So I make an idle boast;
Jesus of the twice-turned cheek,   95
Lamb of God, although I speak
With my mouth thus, in my heart
Do I play a double part.

Ever at Thy glowing altar
Must my heart grow sick and falter,   100
Wishing He I served were black,
Thinking then it would not lack
Precedent of pain to guide it,
Let who would or might deride it;
Surely then this flesh would know   105
Yours had borne a kindred woe.

Lord, I fashion dark gods, too,
Daring even to give You
Dark despairing features where,
Crowned with dark rebellious hair,   110
Patience wavers just so much as
Mortal grief compels, while touches
Quick and hot, of anger, rise
To smitten cheek and weary eyes.
Lord, forgive me if my need   115
Sometimes shapes a human creed.

All day long and all night through,
One thing only must I do:
Quench my pride and cool my blood,
Lest I perish in the flood.   120
Lest a hidden ember set
Timber that I thought was wet
Burning like the dryest flax,
Melting like the merest wax,
Lest the grave restore its dead.   125
Not yet has my heart or head
In the least way realized
They and I are civilized.

Do Not Go Gentle into That Good Night

Dylan Thomas (1914–1953)

Do not go gentle into that good night,
Old age should burn and rave at close of day;
Rage, rage against the dying of the light.

Though wise men at their end know dark is right,
Because their words had forked no lightning they   5
Do not go gentle into that good night.

Good men, the last wave by, crying how bright
Their frail deeds might have danced in a green bay,
Rage, rage against the dying of the light.

Wild men who caught and sang the sun in flight, 10
And learn, too late, they grieved it on its way,
Do not go gentle into that good night.

Grave men, near death, who see with blinding sight
Blind eyes could blaze like meteors and be gay,
Rage, rage against the dying of the light. 15

And you, my father, there on the sad height,
Curse, bless, me now with your fierce tears, I pray.
Do not go gentle into that good night.
Rage, rage against the dying of the light.

Read by the author on *Dylan Thomas Reading* (Caedmon TC-1002 and TC-2014).

Love Calls Us to the Things of This World

Richard Wilbur (1921–   )

The eyes open to a cry of pulleys,
And spirited from sleep, the astounded soul
Hangs for a moment bodiless and simple
As false dawn.
                    Outside the open window
The morning air is all awash with angels. 5

Some are in bed-sheets, some are in blouses,
Some are in smocks: but truly there they are.
Now they are rising together in calm swells
Of halcyon feeling, filling whatever they wear
With the deep joy of their impersonal breathing; 10

Now they are flying in place, conveying
The terrible speed of their omnipresence, moving
And staying like white water; and now of a sudden
They swoon down into so rapt a quiet
That nobody seems to be there.
                            The soul shrinks 15

From all that it is about to remember,
From the punctual rape of every blessèd day,

"Love Calls Us to the Things of This World" from *Things of This World* © 1956 by Richard Wilbur. Reprinted by permission of Harcourt Brace Jovanovich, Inc.

And cries,
            "Oh, let there be nothing on earth but laundry,
Nothing but rosy hands in the rising steam
And clear dances done in the sight of heaven."   20

   Yet, as the sun acknowledges
With a warm look the world's hunks and colors,
The soul descends once more in bitter love
To accept the waking body, saying now
In a changed voice as the man yawns and rises,   25

   "Bring them down from their ruddy gallows;
Let there be clean linen for the backs of thieves;
Let lovers go fresh and sweet to be undone,
And the heaviest nuns walk in a pure floating
Of dark habits,
            keeping their difficult balance."   30

Read by the author on *The Caedmon Treasury of Modern Poets* (Caedmon TC-2006).

Big John Henry

Margaret Walker (1915–   )

This here's a tale of a sho-nuff man
Whut lived one time in the delta lan'.
His hand was big as a hog's fat ham
And he useta work for Uncle Sam.
His gums was blue, his voice was mellow   5
And he talked to mules, fellow to fellow.
The day he was born in the Mississippi bottom
He made a meal on buttermilk and sorghum
A mess o' peas and a bait o' tunnips
And when he finished he smacked his lips   10
And went outside to help pick cotton.
And he growed up taller than a six-foot shooter
Skinnin' mules and catchin' barracuda
And stronger than a team of oxen
And he even could beat the champion boxin'   15
An' ain't nary man in Dixie's forgotten
How he could raise two bales of cotton
While one hand anchored down the steamboat.

"Big John Henry" from *For My People* by Margaret Walker. Copyright © 1942 by Yale University Press. Reprinted by permission.

Oh, they ain't no tale was ever wrote
'Bout Big John Henry that could start to tell   20
All the things that Big Boy knowed so well:
How he learned to whistle from the whippoorwills,
And turned the wheels whut ran the mills;
How the witches taught him how to cunjer,
And cyo the colic and ride the thunder;   25
And how he made friends with a long lean houn'
Sayin', "It's jes' John Henry a-giftin' 'roun'."
But a ten-poun' hammer done ki-ilt John Henry
Yeah, a ten-poun' hammer ki-ilt John Henry,
Bust him open, wide Lawd!   30
Drapped him ovah, wide Lawd!
Po' John Henry, he cold and dead.

Read by the author on *Anthology of Negro Poets* (Folkways FL-9791).

Seven

The Poets' Revisions

In discussing the many poems you have read thus far, you have probably wondered more than once what the limits of reasonable interpretation are. At what point are we merely being clever or ingenious or overly subtle, reading into a poem much more than the poet could possibly (or probably) have meant to put into it. The question is legitimate and inevitable but extremely difficult to answer satisfactorily. If anything should be clear at this point, it is that poetry, by its very nature, does not yield itself to clear, definitive interpretations. The poet strives for richness of expression, and expresses himself in a figurative language whose very purpose is to convey complex ideas, attitudes, and emotions in sensuous and concrete imagery. In discussing poems in class, you have no doubt benefited from the insights of your fellow students (and no doubt benefited them with yours). In re-reading a poem you like, you have probably discovered new things about the poem with each re-reading. In fact, when we judge a particular poem to be good or great the poem is almost certainly one that stands up and indeed improves—or at least our understanding of it improves—with each re-reading.

This is not to say that interpretation of a poem is entirely a subjective affair or that one interpretation is as good as another. We obviously cannot accept two mutually contradictory interpretations of a poem. We must decide, for example, whether the duke in Browning's "My Last Duchess" is a loving husband who was wronged by his former wife or is a vain and proud man who wronged her. But the problem arises not so much over matters of fundamental meaning as over the limits that ought to be placed on interpretation. To come back, then, to our original question: How can we know if we are over-reading, putting into the poem things the author never intended to be there? One answer is that we cannot as a general rule rely on what the poet intends, since in most cases we have no way of determining what the poet's intentions were—most poets are reluctant to discuss their poems—except by reading and analyzing the poem. There is always the danger, of course, that a poem will trigger in us a flight of critical fancy that bears little relationship to the poem itself. But if we are careful readers, constantly mindful that our interpretations must first and last be supported by the poem, the best assumption is that we are responding to the conscious and deliberate artistry of the poet. We are giving him the benefit of the doubt.

One of the popular misconceptions about poetry is that it gets written in a state of blinding, romantic inspiration. The poet is visited by the angel or the demon of inspiration and spills his poem onto paper. Now some poems probably do get written this way, and many more probably begin this way. But between the blinding flash (if that is the form the inspiration takes) and the finished poem, most poets put in a good deal of unromantic hard work. That is to say, most poems are the result of a highly conscious, careful artistry that fully warrants and indeed demands our reading them with care and attention.

The following pages give you an opportunity to examine early drafts and trial stanzas of a number of poems. For purposes of clarity, brackets are used to indicate variants and deletions in a number of poems.

A comparison of these early drafts with the final versions will demonstrate how deliberate and conscious the act of poetic creation is.

A Noiseless Patient Spider

Walt Whitman (1819–1892)

Final version, 1871

A noiseless patient spider,
I mark'd where on a little promontory it stood isolated,
Mark'd how to explore the vacant vast surrounding,
It launch'd forth filament, filament, filament, out of itself,
Ever unreeling them, ever tirelessly speeding them.   5

And you O my soul where you stand,
Surrounded, detached, in measureless oceans of space,
Ceaselessly musing, venturing, throwing, seeking the spheres to
      connect them,
Till the bridge you will need be form'd, till the ductile anchor hold,
Till the gossamer thread you fling catch somewhere, O my soul.   10

Notebook version, early 1860s

The Soul, reaching, throwing out for love,
As the spider, from some little promontory, throwing out filament after
    filament, tirelessly out of itself, that one at least may catch and form
    a link, a bridge, a connection
O I saw one passing along, saying hardly a word—yet full of love
    I detected him, by certain signs
O eyes wishfully turning! O silent eyes!
For then I thought of you oer the world   5
O latent oceans, fathomless oceans of love!
O waiting oceans of love! yearning and fervid! and of you sweet souls
    perhaps in the future, delicious and long:
But Dead, unknown on the earth—ungiven, dark here, unspoken, never born:
You fathomless latent souls of love—you pent and unknown oceans of love!

**She Dwelt
among the Untrodden Ways**

William Wordsworth (1770–1850)

Final version, 1800

She dwelt among the untrodden ways
    Beside the springs of Dove,
A maid whom there were none to praise
    And very few to love:

A violet by a mossy stone   5
    Half hidden from the eye!
—Fair as a star, when only one
    Is shining in the sky.

She lived unknown, and few could know
    When Lucy ceased to be;   10
But she is in her grave, and, oh,
    The difference to me!

237

First version, 1798 or 1799

My hope was one, from cities far
   Nursed on a lonesome heath:
Her lips were red as roses are,
   Her hair a woodbine wreath.

She lived among the untrodden ways   5
   Beside the springs of Dove,
A maid whom there were none to praise,
   And very few to love;

A violet by a mossy stone
   Half-hidden from the eye!   10
Fair as a star when only one
   Is shining in the sky!

And she was graceful as the broom
   That flowers by Carron's side;
But slow distemper checked her bloom,   15
   And on the Heath she died.

Long time before her head lay low
   Dead to the world was she:
But now she's in her grave, and Oh!
   The difference to me!   20

An Elementary School Classroom in a Slum

Stephen Spender (1909–   )

As revised for <u>Collected Poems,</u> 1941

Far far from gusty waves, these children's faces.
Like rootless weeds the torn hair round their paleness.
The tall girl with her weighed-down head. The paper-
seeming boy with rat's eyes. The stunted unlucky heir
Of twisted bones, reciting a father's gnarled disease,   5
His lesson from his desk. At back of the dim class,
One unnoted, sweet and young: his eyes live in a dream
Of squirrels' game, in tree room, other than this.

On sour cream walls, donations. Shakespeare's head
Cloudless at dawn, civilized dome riding all cities.   10
Belled, flowery, Tyrolese valley. Open-handed map
Awarding the world its world. And yet, for these
Children, these windows, not this world, are world,
Where all their future's painted with a fog,
A narrow street sealed in with a lead sky,   15
Far far from rivers, capes, and stars of words.

Surely Shakespeare is wicked, the map a bad example
With ships and sun and love tempting them to steal —
For lives that slyly turn in their cramped holes
From fog to endless night? On their slag heap, these children   20
Wear skins peeped through by bones and spectacles of steel
With mended glass, like bottle bits on stones.
All of their time and space are foggy slum
So blot their maps with slums as big as doom.

Unless, governor, teacher, inspector, visitor,   25
This map becomes their window and these windows
That open on their lives like crouching tombs
Break, O break open, till they break the town
And show the children to the fields and all their world
Azure on their sands, to let their tongues   30
Run naked into books, the white and green leaves open
The history theirs whose language is the sun.

**Original version, as published in <u>London Mercury</u>, May 1935
(titled "An Elementary School Classroom")**

Far far from gusty waves, these children's faces.
Like rootless weeds the torn hair round their paleness.
The tall girl with her weighed-down head. The paper-
seeming boy with rat's eyes. The stunted unlucky heir
Of twisted bones, reciting a father's gnarled disease,   5
His lesson from his desk. At back of the dim class
One unnoted, mild and young: his eyes live in a dream
Of squirrel's game, in tree room, other than this.

On sour cream walls, donations. Shakespeare's head
Cloudless at dawn, civilized dome riding all cities.   10
Belled, flowery, Tyrolese valley. Open-handed map
Awarding the explicit world, of every name but here.

Original version reprinted by permission of Random House, Inc. and Faber and Faber Ltd.

To few, too few, these are real windows: world and words and waving
Leaves, to heal. For these young lives, guilty and dangerous
Is fantasy of travel. Surely, Shakespeare is wicked.   15

To lives that wryly turn, under the structural Lie,
Toward smiles or hate? Amongst their heap, these children
Wear skins peeped through by bones, and spectacles of steel
With mended glass, like bottle bits in slag.
Tyrol is wicked; map's promising a fable: 20
All of their time and space are foggy slum,
So blot their maps with slums as big as doom.

Unless, dowager, governor, these pictures, in a room
Columned above childishness, like our day's future drift
Of smoke concealing war, are voices shouting   25
O that beauty has words and works which break
Through coloured walls and towers. The children stand
As in a climbing mountain train. This lesson illustrates
The world green in their many valleys beneath:
The total summer heavy with their flowers.   30

Lenore

Edgar Allan Poe (1809–1849)

Final version, 1845

Ah, broken is the golden bowl! the spirit flown forever!
Let the bell toll! — a saintly soul floats on the Stygian river;
And, Guy De Vere, hast *thou* no tear? — weep now or never more!
See on yon drear and rigid bier low lies thy love, Lenore!
Come! let the burial rite be read — the funeral song be sung! —   5
An anthem for the queenliest dead that ever died so young —
A dirge for her the doubly dead in that she died so young.

"Wretches! ye loved her for her wealth and hated her for her pride,
And when she fell in feeble health, ye blessed her — that she died!
How *shall* the ritual, then, be read? — the requiem how be sung   10
By you — by yours, the evil eye, — by yours, the slanderous tongue
That did to death the innocence that died, and died so young?"

Peccavimus; but rave not thus! and let a Sabbath song
Go up to God so solemnly the dead may feel no wrong!
The sweet Lenore hath "gone before," with Hope, that flew beside,   15
Leaving thee wild for the dear child that should have been thy bride —

240

For her, the fair and *debonnaire,* that now so lowly lies,
The life upon her yellow hair but not within her eyes —
The life still there, upon her hair — the death upon her eyes.

"Avaunt! to-night my heart is light. No dirge will I upraise,   20
But waft the angel on her flight with a paean of old days!
Let *no* bell toll! — lest her sweet soul, amid its hallowed mirth,
Should catch the note, as it doth float up from the damnèd Earth.
To friends above, from fiends below, the indignant ghost is riven —
From Hell unto a high estate far up within the Heaven —   25
From grief and groan, to a golden throne, beside the King of Heaven."

Peccavimus (l. 13): Latin, meaning "We have sinned."

First version, 1831 (originally titled "A Paean")

                    I

How shall the burial rite be read?
   The solemn song be sung?
The requiem for the loveliest dead,
   That ever died so young?

                    II

Her friends are gazing on her,   5
   And on her gaudy bier,
And weep! — oh! to dishonor
   Dead beauty with a tear!

                    III

They loved her for her wealth —
   And they hated her for her pride —   10
But she grew in feeble health,
   And they love her — that she died.

                    IV

They tell me (while they speak
   Of her "costly broider'd pall")
That my voice is growing weak —   15
   That I should not sing at all —

Or that my tone should be
   Tun'd to such solemn song
So mournfully—so mournfully,
   That the dead may feel no wrong.   20

VI

But she is gone above,
   With young Hope at her side,
And I am drunk with love
   Of the dead, who is my bride —

VII

Of the dead—dead who lies   25
   All perfum'd there,
With the dead upon her eyes,
   And the life upon her hair.

VIII

Thus on the coffin loud and long
   I strike—the murmur sent   30
Through the grey chambers to my song,
   Shall be the accompaniment.

IX

Thou died'st in thy life's June —
   But thou did'st not die too fair:
Thou did'st not die too soon,   35
   Nor with too calm an air.

X

From more than fiends on earth,
   Thy life and love are riven,
To join the untainted mirth
   Of more than thrones in heaven —   40

XI

Therefore, to thee this night
   I will no requiem raise,
But waft thee on thy flight,
   With a Paean of old days.

Second version, 1843

Ah, broken is the golden bowl!
   The spirit flown forever!
Let the bell toll! — A saintly soul
   Glides down the Stygian river!
And let the burial rite be read —   5
   The funeral song be sung —
A dirge for the most lovely dead
   That ever died so young!
     And, Guy De Vere,
     Hast thou no tear?   10
      Weep now or nevermore!
      See, on yon bier,
       Low lies thy love Lenore!

"Yon heir, whose cheeks of pallid hue
   With tears are streaming wet,   15
Sees only, through
Their crocodile dew,
   A vacant coronet —
    False friends! ye loved her for her wealth
     And hated her for pride,   20
    And, when she fell in feeble health,
     Ye blessed her — that she died.
     How shall the ritual, then, be read?
      The requiem how be sung
       For her most wrong'd of all the dead   25
       That ever died so young?"

Peccavimus!
But rave not thus!
   And let the solemn song
Go up to God so mournfully that she may feel no wrong!   30
    The sweet Lenore
    Hath "gone before"
     With young hope at her side,
     And thou art wild
     For the dear child   35
    That should have been thy bride —
    For her, the fair
    And debonair,
     That now so lowly lies —
    The life still there   40
    Upon her hair,
     The death upon her eyes.

"Avaunt! — to-night
My heart is light —
   No, dirge will I upraise,   45
But waft the angel on her flight
With a Paean of old days!
    Let no bell toll!
    Lest her sweet soul,
      Amid its hallow'd mirth   /   50
      Should catch the note
      As it doth float

Up from the damnèd earth —
To friends above, from fiends below, th' indignant
    ghost is riven —   55
  From grief and moan
  To a gold throne
Beside the King of Heaven!"

Bavarian Gentians

D. H. Lawrence (1885–1930)

Final version, 1932

Not every man has gentians in his house
in Soft September, at slow, sad Michaelmas.

Bavarian gentians, big and dark, only dark
darkening the day-time, torch-like with the smoking blueness of
    Pluto's gloom,
ribbed and torch-like, with their blaze of darkness spread blue   5
down flattening into points, flattened under the sweep of white day
torch-flower of the blue-smoking darkness, Pluto's dark-blue daze,
black lamps from the halls of Dis, burning dark blue,
giving off darkness, blue darkness, as Demeter's pale lamps give off light,
lead me then, lead the way.   10

Reach me a gentian, give me a torch!
let me guide myself with the blue, forked torch of this flower
down the darker and darker stairs, where blue is darkened on blueness

even where Persephone goes, just now, from the frosted September
to the sightless realm where darkness is awake upon the dark   15
and Persephone herself is but a voice
or a darkness invisible enfolded in the deeper dark
of the arms Plutonic, and pierced with the passion of dense gloom,
among the splendour of torches of darkness, shedding darkness on
      the lost bride and her groom.

Early version, 1928?

Not every man has gentians in his house
In soft September, at slow, sad Michaelmas.

Bavarian gentians, tall and dark, but dark
darkening the daytime torch-like with the smoking blueness of Pluto's gloom,
ribbed hellish flowers erect, with their blaze of darkness spread blue,   5
blown flat into points, by the heavy white draught of the day.

Torch-flowers of the blue-smoking darkness, Pluto's dark-blue blaze
black lamps from the halls of Dis, smoking dark blue
giving off darkness, blue darkness, upon Demeter's yellow-pale day
whom have you come for, here in the white-cast day?   10

Reach me a gentian, give me a torch!
let me guide myself with the blue, forked torch of a flower
down the darker and darker stairs, where blue is darkened on blueness
down the way Persephone goes, just now, in first-frosted September.
to the sightless realm where darkness is married to dark   15
and Persephone herself is but a voice, as a bride,
a gloom invisible enfolded in the deeper dark
of the arms of Pluto as he ravishes her once again
and pierces her once more with his passion of the utter dark
among the splendour of black-blue torches, shedding fathomless darkness
      on the nuptials.   20

Give me a flower on a tall stem, and three dark flames,
for I will go to the wedding, and be wedding-guest
at the marriage of the living dark.

245

In White

Robert Frost (1874–1963)

Early version (for final version, see "Design," p. 55)

A dented spider like a snow drop white
On a white Heal-all, holding up a moth
Like a white piece of lifeless satin cloth—
Saw ever curious eye so strange a sight?—
Portent in little, assorted death and blight   5
Like ingredients of a witches' broth?—
The beady spider, the flower like a froth,
And the moth carried like a paper kite.

What had that flower to do with being white,
The blue prunella every child's delight.   10
What brought the kindred spider to that height?
(Make we no thesis of the miller's plight.)
What but design of darkness and of night?
Design, design! Do I use the word aright?

The Tiger

William Blake (1757–1827)

Final version, 1794

Tiger! Tiger! burning bright
In the forests of the night,
What immortal hand or eye
Could frame thy fearful symmetry?

In what distant deeps or skies   5
Burnt the fire of thine eyes?
On what wings dare he aspire?
What the hand dare seize the fire?

And what shoulder, and what art,
Could twist the sinews of thy heart?
And when thy heart began to beat,
What dread hand? and what dread feet?

10

What the hammer? what the chain?
In what furnace was thy brain?
What the anvil? what dread grasp
Dare its deadly terrors clasp?

15

When the stars threw down their spears,
And water'd heaven with their tears,
Did he smile his work to see?
Did he who made the Lamb make thee?

20

Tiger! Tiger! burning bright
In the forests of the night,
What immortal hand or eye
Dare frame thy fearful symmetry?

First draft, 1793

Tyger Tyger burning bright
In the forests of the night
What immortal hand [and] [or] eye
[Could] [Dare] frame thy fearful symmetry

[In what] [Burnt in] distant deeps or skies   5
[Burnt the] [The cruel] fire of thine eyes
On what wings dare he aspire
What the hand dare seize the fire

And what shoulder & what art
Could twist the sinews of thy heart   10
And when thy heart began to beat
What dread hand and what dread feet

[Could fetch it from the furnace deep
And in thy horrid ribs dare steep
In the well of sanguine woe   15
In what clay and in what mould
Were thy eyes of fury rolld]

[What] [Where] the hammer [what] ⌐ ⌐here] the chain
In what furnace was thy brain
What the anvil what [the arm] [arm] [grasp] [clasp] dread grasp   20
[Could] [Dare] its deadly terrors [clasp] [grasp] [clasp]

Tyger Tyger burning bright
In the forests of the night
What immortal hand and eye
Dare [form] [frame] thy fearful symmetry   25

Trial stanzas, 1793

[Burnt in distant deeps or skies
The cruel fire of thine eye,
Could heart descend or wings aspire
What the hand dare seize the fire]

And [did he laugh] dare he [smile] [laugh] his work to see   5
[What the shoulder ankle what the knee]
[Did] [Dare] he who made the lamb make thee
When the stars threw down their spears
And waterd heaven with their tears

Second draft, 1793

Tyger Tyger burning bright
In the forests of the night
What Immortal hand [or] [and] eye
Dare frame thy fearful symmetry

And what shoulder and what art   5
Could twist the sinews of thy heart
And when thy heart began to beat
What dread hand and what dread feet

When the stars threw down their spears
And watered heaven with their tears   10
Did he smile his work to see
Did he who made the lamb make thee

Tyger Tyger burning bright
In the forests of the night
What immortal hand and eye   15
Dare frame thy fearful symmetry

To an Athlete Dying Young

A. E. Housman (1859–1936)

Final version, 1896

The time you won your town the race
We chaired you through the market-place;
Man and boy stood cheering by,
And home we brought you shoulder-high.

To-day, the road all runners come,   5
Shoulder-high we bring you home,
And set you at your threshold down,
Townsman of a stiller town.

Smart lad, to slip betimes away
From fields where glory does not stay   10
And early though the laurel grows
It withers quicker than the rose.

Eyes the shady night has shut
Cannot see the record cut,
And silence sounds no worse than cheers   15
After earth has stopped the ears:

Now you will not swell the rout
Of lads that wore their honours out,
Runners whom renown outran
And the name died before the man.   20

So set, before its echoes fade,
The fleet foot on the sill of shade,
And hold to the low lintel up
The still-defended challenge-cup.

And round that early-laurelled head   25
Will flock to gaze the strengthless dead.
And find unwithered on its curls
The garland briefer than a girl's.

First draft, 1895

That day you won [the] your town the race
[They] We chaired you [in] through the market-place,
[And here the crowd] [Where market folk] stood cheering by,
And [home] home we brought you shoulder high.

So now with ribboned breast invade   5
[So, now, with laurels undecayed]
        [before the laurels fade]
        [unbeaten, unafraid]
First in the race, the sill of shade
[So set, before its echoes fade,]   10
[Set foot upon the sill of shade]
And hold the [dark] low lintel up
The still defended challenge-cup.

Wise lad, to steal betimes away
From fields where victory will not stay   15
A garland briefer than a girl's [maid's]
Now the eye that night has shut
And never see your record cut.

And round your early-laurelled [that young and laurelled] head
Will throng to gaze [come and gaze] the strengthless dead,   20
And yet unfaded round its [find unwithered on] curls
Your [The] garland briefer than a girl's.

Of runners whom renown outran
And [Or] the name died before the man.

Second draft, 1895

The [day] time you won your town the race
We chaired you through the market-place;
Man and boy stood cheering by,
And home we brought you shoulder-high.

Today, the road all runners come,   5
Shoulder-high we bring you home,
And set you at your threshold down,
Townsman of a stiller town.

Wise lad [Well done,] [Smart lad,] to slip betimes away
From fields where glory [victory] will not stay   10
[And glory for the runner braids]
[And early though the laurel grows]
[A chaplet briefer than a maid's]
It withers sooner [lasts no longer] than [the] a rose.

The man [He] whose eye the night has shut   15
Eyes the shady [cloudy] night has shut
[Never sees his record cut]
[Will never see]
[Never see the record cut]
And silence sounds no worse than [is the same as] cheers   20
After earth has stopped the [his] ears.

[And] Now you will [have] not join [swelled] the throng
Of lads that lived [stayed] a spell [day] too long,
Runners whom renown outran
And the name died before the man.   25

Anthem for Doomed Youth

Wilfred Owen (1893–1918)

Final version, 1917

What passing-bells for these who die as cattle?
   Only the monstrous anger of the guns.
   Only the stuttering rifles' rapid rattle
Can patter out their hasty orisons.
No mockeries now for them; no prayers nor bells,   5
   Nor any voice of mourning save the choirs—
The shrill, demented choirs of wailing shells;
   And bugles calling for them from sad shires.

What candles may be held to speed them all?
   Not in the hands of boys, but in their eyes   10
Shall shine the holy glimmers of good-byes.
   The pallor of girls' brows shall be their pall;
Their flowers the tenderness of patient minds,
And each slow dusk a drawing-down of blinds.

"Anthem for Doomed Youth" from Wilfred Owen, *Collected Poems*. Copyright Chatto & Windus Ltd. 1946, © 1963. Final version, first and second drafts reprinted by permission of New Directions Publishing Corporation, Chatto and Windus Ltd., and Mr. Harold Owen.

First draft, 1917 (originally titled "Anthem for Dead Youth")

What passing-bells for these who die so fast?
  —Only the monstrous anger of our guns.
Let the majestic insults of their iron mouths
  Be as the requiem of their burials.
Of choristers and holy music, none;   5
  Nor any voice of mourning, save the wail
The long-drawn wail of high far-sailing shells.

What candles may we hold to light these lost?
  —Not in the hands of boys, but in their eyes
Shall shine the many flames: holy candles.   10
  Women's wide-spread arms shall be their wreaths,
And pallor of girls' cheeks shall be their palls.
  Their flowers, the tenderness of rough men's minds.
And each slow Dusk, a drawing-down of blinds.

Second draft, 1917 (originally titled "Anthem for Dead Youth")

What passing-bells for you who die in herds?
  —Only the monstrous anger of the guns!
  —Only the stuttering rifles' rattled words
Can patter out your hasty orisons.
No chants for you, nor balms, nor wreaths, nor bells,   5
  Nor any voice of mourning, save the choirs,
And long-drawn sighs of wailing shells;
  And bugles calling for you from sad shires.

What candles may we hold to speed you all?
  Not in the hands of boys, but in their eyes   10
Shall shine [the] holy lights of our goodbyes.
  The pallor of girls' brows must be your pall.
Your flowers, the tenderness of comrades' minds,
And each slow dusk, a drawing-down of blinds.

The Second Coming

W. B. Yeats (1865–1939)

Final version, 1921

Turning and turning in the widening gyre
The falcon cannot hear the falconer;
Things fall apart; the centre cannot hold;
Mere anarchy is loosed upon the world,
The blood-dimmed tide is loosed, and everywhere   5
The ceremony of innocence is drowned;
The best lack all conviction, while the worst
Are full of passionate intensity.

Surely some revelation is at hand;
Surely the Second Coming is at hand.   10
The Second Coming! Hardly are those words out
When a vast image out of *Spiritus Mundi*
Troubles my sight: somewhere in sands of the desert
A shape with lion body and the head of a man,
A gaze blank and pitiless as the sun,   15
Is moving its slow thighs, while all about it
Reel shadows of the indignant desert birds.
The darkness drops again; but now I know
That twenty centuries of stony sleep
Were vexed to nightmare by a rocking cradle,   20
And what rough beast, its hour come round at last,
Slouches towards Bethlehem to be born?

Spiritus Mundi (l. 12): Soul of the universe, which Yeats believed constituted a fund of racial memories and images.

First full draft, 1919

Turning and turning in the wide gyre [widening gyre]
The falcon cannot hear the falconer
[Things fall apart, the centre has lost]
Things fall apart—the centre cannot hold
[Vile] Mere anarchy is loose there on the world   5

The blood stained flood [dim tide] is loose and anarchy
[The good are wavering and intensity]
The best [lose] lack all conviction while the worst
Are full of passionate intensity.

Surely some revelation is at hand   10
[The cradle at Bethlehem has rocked must leap anew]
[Surely the great falcon must come]
[Surely the hour of the second birth is here]
[Surely the hour of the second birth has struck]
[The second Birth! Scarce have those] words been spoken   15
The second [Birth] coming. [Scarce have the words been spoken]
[Before the dark was cut as with a knife]
And new intensity rent as it were cloth
And a [stark] lost image out of spiritus mundi
Troubles my sight. [A waste of sand] — A waste of desert sand   20
A shape with lion's body & with and the head [breast and head] of a man
[An eye] A gaze blank and pitiless as the sun
[Move with a slow slouching step]
Moves its slow [feet] thighs while all about its head
[An angry crowd of desert]   25
[Fall] [Run] shadows of the [desert birds they] indignant desert birds
The darkness drops again but now I know
[For] That twenty centuries of [its] stony sleep
[Were vexed & all but broken by the second]
Were vexed to nightmare by a rocking cradle   30
[And now at last]
[And now at last knowing its hour come round]
And what [at last] [wild thing] rough beast its hour come round at last
        knowing the hour [come round]
[It slouches towards Bethlehem to be born]
It has set out for Bethlehem to be born   35
It has set out for Bethlehem to be born
[Is slouching] towards Bethlehem to be born
Slouches towards Bethlehem to be born.

First draft reprinted by permission of M. B. Yeats and Anne Yeats.

Glossary

Allegory   A form of symbolism in which concepts and abstract qualities are represented as persons. The situations in allegory are generally narrative and dramatic, leading to some moral or philosophic statement.
   Emily Dickinson, [Apparently with no surprise], p. 55
   John Keats, To Autumn, p. 61

Alliteration   Repetition within a phrase or line of an initial consonant sound in two or more words (e.g., wild and woolly, footloose and fancy free).
   Louis Simpson, As Birds Are Fitted to the Boughs (l. 3), p. 44
   Traditional, Barbara Allen (l. 5), p. 165
   Stephen Stills, Suite: Judy Blue Eyes (l. 49), p. 197

Allusion   A reference, often implied or indirect, to something famous outside the poem, such as a person, event, or story.
   Robert Frost, Out, Out—, p. 75
   E. Curmie Price, The Ballad of Bigger Thomas, p. 60

Apostrophe   A figure of speech in which the speaker of a poem directly addresses a person who is dead or absent, an abstract quality, or a *personification*.
   William Blake, The Tiger, p. 246
   W. B. Yeats, Sailing to Byzantium (3rd stanza), p. 57
   John Donne, [Batter my heart, three-personed God], p. 66

Assonance   Repetition within a phrase or line of a vowel in two or more words when surrounding consonants are different (e.g., read and weep, laugh last).
   Christina Rossetti, A Birthday (ll. 6–8), p. 44
   Robert Herrick, Upon Julia's Clothes (l. 2), p. 26
   Langston Hughes, Same in Blues (l. 7), p. 225

255

Ballad   A narrative or dramatic poem that usually focuses on a climactic episode through which the larger action is implied. Folk ballads are thought to be communal in origin and are transmitted orally, a process that has resulted in variations of a single ballad. A common form of the ballad is an alternate 4- and 3-stress line, rhyming abcb.

Traditional, The Unquiet Grave, p. 167
Traditional, Lord Randall, p. 162
Dudley Randall, Ballad of Birmingham, p. 190

Blank verse   Lines of unrhymed iambic pentameter (see *meter*). Since it comes closer to the rhythm of ordinary speech than any other traditional verse form, blank verse has been widely used in dramatic poetry.

Robert Frost, "Out, Out—," p. 75
Stephen Spender, The Express, p. 114
Wallace Stevens, Of Modern Poetry, p. 18

Caesura   A pronounced pause within a line (see *Meter*).

Carpe diem   A Latin phrase meaning "seize the day," characterizing lyric poems that urge the reader or (often) a young lady to make the most of, say, beauty and youth before the swift onset of death.

Andrew Marvell, To His Coy Mistress, p. 50
Robert Herrick, To Daffodils, p. 45

Chorus   (See *Refrain*.)

Connotation   The associative or suggestive meanings of a word in contrast to its denotative or literal meaning.

Consonance   Repetition of a consonant sound (but not of a vowel) at the ends of two or more stressed syllables in a phrase or line (e.g., pick and pack, tip-top).

Lewis Carroll, Jabberwocky (l. 18), p. 38
Edgar Allan Poe, Lenore (ll. 5, 24), p. 240
William Jay Smith, American Primitive (l. 5), p. 101
William Carlos Williams, The Dance (ll. 4, 7), p. 137

Convention   Any form, style, or treatment of a particular kind of subject matter that appears repeatedly over a period of time. When we speak of the *ballad* convention, we usually mean a narrative poem that focuses on a climactic event, written in *quatrains* of alternate 4- and 3-stress lines and often including a *refrain* or chorus. We can speak of the convention of the *sonnet* in formal terms (fourteen lines of iambic pentameter with a particular rhyme scheme) or in terms of subject matter and treatment. During the Elizabethan period in England, the sonnet was used frequently by men to praise and flatter young ladies in what rapidly became standard, conventional comparisons.

Henry Constable, [My lady's presence makes the roses red], p. 124
William Shakespeare, [My mistress' eyes are nothing like the sun], p. 124
John Keats, On First Looking into Chapman's Homer, p. 54

256

Couplet   Two successive rhyming lines of verse with the same *meter*. The closed couplet designates two rhyming, *end-stopped* lines (see *Meter*).

Denotation   The literal, dictionary meaning of a word in contrast to its connotative or suggestive meaning.

Diction   The choice of words in a work. Although in the past poets and critics have developed rather precise rules about the poetic diction appropriate to different types or subjects of poetry, the tendency of modern poetry has been to ignore rigid formulations and rules in favor of greater freedom.

Didactic   Having as its main purpose to instruct or teach, usually in matters of morality, ethics, or religion. The term is often used to express a derogatory judgment, as a shorthand way of saying that the artist is more interested in teaching a lesson than in creating an artistically satisfying work. However, used descriptively and neutrally, the term is valuable in describing works that, while generally acknowledged to be artistic successes, nevertheless make statements about morality, ethics, religion, politics, etc.
  Wilfred Owen, Dulce et Decorum Est, p. 91
  Ben Jonson, [Doing, a filthy pleasure is, and short], p. 67

Dramatic monologue   A poem in which the speaker addresses one or more silent listeners at some crucial moment in his life and thereby reveals, perhaps unwittingly, the nature of his personality. The poem is dramatic in that the speaker, a fictional or historical figure, is speaking at a particular time and place about a matter of deep concern to him; it is a monologue in that the speaker's is the only voice we hear.
  Robert Browning, My Last Duchess, p. 68
  T. S. Eliot, The Love Song of J. Alfred Prufrock, p. 211

Elegy   A mournful, melancholy, or plaintive poem, especially a funeral song or a lament for the dead.
  James Wright, Paul, p. 76
  Thomas Gray, Elegy Written in a Country Churchyard, p. 78
  William Bell, On a Dying Boy, p. 77

End rhyme   A verse in which rhyming words occur at the ends of lines.

End-stopped   Terminating a phrase, clause, or sentence, as at the end of a line or *couplet* (see *Meter*).

Figurative language   A general term covering the many devices in which language is used nonliterally, or in which comparisons are made between essentially dissimilar things. (See *Metaphor, Metonymy, Paradox, Simile, Symbol, Synecdoche.*)

Foot   (See *Meter*.)

257

Free verse   Poetry "freed" from the restriction of rhythmic and metric regularity, usually unrhymed. Freed from these restrictions, the poet relies on patterns of *imagery*, repetition, *parallelism, alliteration,* and other devices to achieve unity.

  LeRoi Jones, The Liar, p. 65
  Walt Whitman, To a Locomotive in Winter, p. 113

Hyperbole   Exaggeration; overstatement.

Imagery   Most commonly, the use of concrete, vivid details to appeal to our sense of sight, sound, smell, taste, or touch.

  Ezra Pound, In a Station of the Metro, p. 74
  William Carlos Williams, The Red Wheelbarrow, p. 75
  Padraic Pearse, Last Lines, p. 59

Irony   The use of language in such a way that the real meaning is different from or opposite to the literal meaning. Verbal irony may take the form of overstatement (or *hyperbole*), in which something is deliberately described in excessive terms; understatement, in which something is deliberately described with less emphasis than is expected; or opposite statement, in which something is described in terms exactly opposed to what is expected. Irony of situation results when there is a discrepancy between what is expected and what actually happens. Dramatic irony, usually found in poems employing such dramatic devices as plot and character, occurs when the reader knows things a character is ignorant of or when a character is unaware that his words and actions reveal him as someone different from what he thinks he is.

  Nigel Dennis, A Desperate Measure, p. 102
  John Crowe Ransom, Bells for John Whiteside's Daughter, p. 82
  Stephen Crane, War Is Kind, p. 69
  Edwin Arlington Robinson, Miniver Cheevy, p. 100
  Robert Browning, My Last Duchess, p. 68

Lyric   Originally, a poem meant to be sung or recited to the accompaniment of a lyre; now, a brief poem expressing the thought or feeling of a single speaker (in contrast to narrative or dramatic poetry).

Metaphor   A figure of speech in which one thing (object, quality, idea) is said to be another, essentially unlike thing.

  Gwendolyn Brooks, Martin Luther King, Jr., p. 47
  John Donne, A Valediction: Forbidding Mourning, p. 51
  Emily Dickinson, [Hope is a subtle glutton], p. 54

Meter   The recurring pattern of accented and unaccented (or stressed and unstressed) syllables in a line of verse. A foot designates one of the four common patterns in English: iambic—an unaccented syllable followed by an accented syllable (device, afraid); trochaic—an accented syllable followed by an unaccented syllable (border, phantom); anapestic—two unaccented syllables followed by one accented syllable (serenade, Tennessee); dactylic — an accented syllable followed by two unaccented syllables (metrical, syllable). A fifth pattern, spondaic, consists of two equally accented syllables (outcome, lifeguard). Since it obviously cannot serve as the prevailing meter in a poem, the spondaic foot is used for variation.

A line of poetry is designated as follows, depending on how many feet it contains: monometer — one foot; dimeter — two feet; trimeter — three feet; tetrameter — four feet; pentameter — five feet; hexameter — six feet. Thus an iambic line of five feet is called iambic pentameter. Scansion is the process of going through a poem, line by line, to determine the prevailing meter. The first stanza of Roy Campbell's "Autumn" (p. 27) scans as follows:

I love|to see,|when leaves|depart,|
The clear|anatomy|arrive,|
Winter,|the paragon|of art,|
That kills|all forms|of life|and feeling|
Save what|is pure|and will|survive.|

The basic foot is iambic and all of the lines contain four feet. The prevailing meter, then, is iambic tetrameter. In line 3, however, the poet has substituted a trochaic foot and in line 4 he has added an unaccented syllable at the end of the line (a line that ends with an unaccented syllable has a feminine ending, and one that ends with an accented syllable has a masculine ending). A pronounced pause within a line, such as occurs after "see" (l. 1) and after Winter (l. 3), is called a *caesura*. Both of these lines are *end-stopped*; that is, each ends with a complete phrase or clause. The next two lines of "Autumn" are:

Already now the clanging chains
Of geese are harnessed to the moon

These lines are said to be *run-on*, since the phrase of the first line runs on into the second line (the noun "chains" is separated from its prepositional modifier "Of geese").

Metonymy   A figure of speech in which a word stands for something closely associated with it, e.g., "I am reading Shakespeare," where Shakespeare means his works. A special form of metonymy is synecdoche, where a part stands for the whole, e.g., "He owns fifty head of cattle."
   Edwin Arlington Robinson, Richard Cory (ll. 13–14), p. 34
   e. e. cummings, i sing of Olaf glad and big (l. 20), p. 35

Octave   A *stanza*, or portion of a stanza, of eight lines (see *Sonnet*).

Onomatopoeia   The use of words whose sounds imitate natural sounds (e.g., bow-wow, cuckoo, babble, gargle).

Paradox   A statement that seems contradictory or absurd but that is nonetheless true or tenable.

Chidiock Tichbourne, Elegy . . . , p. 63
Ralph Waldo Emerson, Brahma, p. 64
John Donne, [Batter my heart, three-personed God], p. 66

Personification   A figure of speech in which inanimate objects or abstract ideas are represented as persons or are given some human attributes.

Victor Hernandez Cruz, today is a day of great joy, p. 4
Henry Constable, [My lady's presence makes the roses red], p. 124
Paul Simon, The Sound of Silence, p. 177

Quatrain   Four successive lines of verse, usually rhyming in alternate lines and having some metric pattern, often a *stanza*.

Refrain   A phrase or verse recurring at intervals in a poem, especially at the end of each *stanza;* a chorus.

Rhyme   The correspondence, in two or more words, between the sounds of the final accented vowel and any following sounds. If at least one of the words occurs within a line, the rhyme is said to be internal. An imperfect or incomplete correspondence of sounds produces near rhyme.

Michael Hamburger, A Poet's Progress, p. 17
James Wright, Paul, p. 76
e. e. cummings, my father moved through dooms of love, p. 208

Rhythm   The alternation of heavy and light stresses in language. Regular alternation produces *meter;* irregular alternation is a characteristic of *free verse.*

Satire   A form of writing that attacks the follies or vices of men. Like ridicule and sarcasm, satire is comic, but unlike them, it exposes weaknesses in order to correct them.

Emily Dickinson, [What soft, cherubic creatures], p. 99
e. e. cummings, the Cambridge ladies who live in furnished souls, p. 100
W. B. Yeats, The Scholars, p. 102

Scansion   (See *Meter.*)

Sestet   A *stanza,* or portion of a stanza, of six lines (see *Sonnet*).

Simile   A figure of speech expressing similarity between two usually dissimilar things, the comparison effected by "like" or "as."

Richard Wilbur, A Simile for Her Smile, p. 43
Joseph Campbell, The Old Woman, p. 43
Henry King, Sic Vita, p. 45

Sonnet   A conventional verse form of fourteen lines of iambic pentameter. The two major types are the Petrarchan (or Italian) and the Shakespearean (or English). The Petrarchan sonnet is divided into an octave (the first eight lines, rhymed abbaabba) and a sestet (the final six lines, rhymed cdecde or cdcdcd). This two-part structure allows the poet to introduce an experience, a problem, a question, or a doubt in the octave and then move to a solution or resolution in the sestet.

The Shakespearean sonnet divides the fourteen lines into three quatrains and a concluding couplet, the rhyme scheme being abab cdcd efef gg. Usually, the first quatrain establishes the theme and the second and third in some way advance, develop, or illustrate it. The final couplet serves variously as insight, discovery, summary, or ironic reversal.

William Shakespeare, [My mistress' eyes are nothing like the sun], p. 124
John Keats, On First Looking into Chapman's Homer, p. 54
Phyllis McGinley, Country Club Sunday, p. 126

Stanza   A group of lines usually arranged in a definite and recurring pattern of *meter* and *rhyme*. Some stanza forms have been used so often they have been given special names, e.g., the *couplet* (two lines) and the *quatrain* (four lines). Such terms can also be used to designate portions of a complexly metered stanza (see *Sonnet*). Irregular patterns, usually found in *free verse,* are designated *verse paragraphs* rather than stanzas.

Symbol   An object or image evoking a cluster of related meanings. Perhaps the most important use of the symbol is that it allows the poet to deal with complex abstractions and relationships through the use of concrete and sensuous *imagery.* Although the line cannot be rigidly drawn, it is useful to distinguish between conventional (or public) symbols and contextual symbols. Conventional symbols are those objects, events, or people that history has invested with meanings now well known; contextual symbols are those whose significance emerges from the poet's treatment within the poem.

William Blake, The Tiger
W. B. Yeats, Sailing to Byzantium
John Drinkwater, Symbols

Synecdoche   (See *Metonymy.*)

Theme   The central or dominating idea of a work. A description of a poem's theme should include not only the subject of the poem but a statement about the manner in which the subject is treated. It is important not to confuse theme with subject. For example, the subject of Robert Frost's "Design" (p. 55) is a moth caught in a spider's web but the theme is the question: is there order and meaning in the universe?

Tone   The general or overall attitude that a writer takes toward his subject. Thus we might describe the tone of a poem as happy, sad, joyful, ironic, solemn, or informal. The term is useful, but since it is a kind of shorthand for the sum of all the parts of a poem, readers will often disagree about the precise tone of a particular poem.

Verse paragraph   A unit of *free verse,* corresponding to the stanza of structured verse.

Author Index

262

Title Index

263

Index of First Lines

267